To Edie,

Thanks so much for coming out tonight.

Keep the light of reason shining!

—Adam Lee

Meta

Meta

On God, the Big Questions, and the Just City
(An Uncommon Exchange)

*Andrew Murtagh
& Adam Lee*

Foreword by *William Jaworski*

CASCADE *Books* • Eugene, Oregon

META
On God, the Big Questions, and the Just City (An Uncommon Exchange)

Copyright © 2017 Wipf and Stock Publishers. All rights reserved. Except for brief quotations in critical publications or reviews, no part of this book may be reproduced in any manner without prior written permission from the publisher. Write: Permissions, Wipf and Stock Publishers, 199 W. 8th Ave., Suite 3, Eugene, OR 97401.

Cascade Books
An Imprint of Wipf and Stock Publishers
199 W. 8th Ave., Suite 3
Eugene, OR 97401

www.wipfandstock.com

PAPERBACK ISBN: 978-1-5326-0347-1
HARDCOVER ISBN: 978-1-5326-0349-5
EBOOK ISBN: 978-1-5326-0348-8

Cataloguing-in-Publication data:

Names: Murtagh, Andrew. | Lee, Adam.

Title: Meta : on God, the big questions, and the just city (an uncommon exchange) / Andrew Murtagh and Adam Lee.

Description: Eugene, OR: Cascade Books, 2017 | Includes bibliographical references.

Identifiers: ISBN 978-1-5326-0347-1 (paperback) | ISBN 978-1-5326-0349-5 (hardcover) | ISBN 978-1-5326-0348-8 (ebook)

Subjects: LCSH: Philosophy. | Ethics. | Justice. | Title.

Classification: BJ1253. M90 2017 (print) | BJ1253 (ebook)

Manufactured in the U.S.A.   DECEMBER 4, 2017

(Murtagh): For Nick. You have inspired. Keep going . . .

(Lee): To my son, Benjamin, and for the world I want to make for you.

Table of Contents

Foreword by William Jaworski ix

Introduction xvii

Round 1: Opening Statements 1

Round 2: Faith, Reason, and Morality, Part I 7

Round 3: Faith, Reason, and Morality, Part II 16

Round 4: Metamorality and Applied Ethics, Part I 24

Round 5: Metamorality and Applied Ethics, Part II 32

Round 6: Philosophical Theism and Christianity, Part I 42

Round 7: Philosophical Theism and Christianity, Part II 54

Round 8: A/theological and Metaphysical Puzzles, Part I 65

Round 9: A/theological and Metaphysical Puzzles, Part II 78

Round 10: A/theological and Metaphysical Puzzles, Part III 91

Round 11: From Metaphysics to Natural Rights and Abortion, Part I 106

Table of Contents

Round 12: From Metaphysics to Natural Rights and Abortion, Part II 116

Round 13: From Metaphysics to Natural Rights and Abortion, Part III 126

Round 14: The Just City: Healthcare, Equal Opportunity, and the Problem of Motivation, Part I 140

Round 15: The Just City: Healthcare, Equal Opportunity, and the Problem of Motivation, Part II 150

Round 16: Closing Statements 161

Bibliography 173

Foreword

Meta is a welcome contribution to the philosophical literature. It is not written by professional philosophers, but by two friends who take seriously Socrates's dictum that the unexamined life is not worth living. In this lies both its charm and its significance, for the authors, Andrew Murtagh and Adam Lee, provide a model of how conversations in day-to-day life can be touched by the philosophical spirit—one that seeks actual reasons for accepting or rejecting various claims, that acknowledges the limitations of one's own perspective, and that is open to altering one's views in the evolving endeavor to discern what is true and to order one's life accordingly.

Professional philosophy tends to be highly rigorous and specialized. The kinds of claims and arguments professional philosophers advance are carefully crafted with an eye to precision and accuracy, and for that reason their work is often inaccessible to nonspecialists—even those with philosophical backgrounds. The upshot is that the books and articles professional philosophers write often do very little to help ordinary people sort through the questions and concerns they have about morality, God, free will, and the human mind. *Meta* provides a refreshing break from philosophy written in the professional mode. It is clear, accessible, and relevant. It represents the kind of attitude that those of us who practice philosophy professionally hope to embody in our research, and that we hope will rub off on our students. To play on a quote from Winston Churchill: we need professional philosophers in the world, but we don't want a world of professional philosophers. What we need are people in all walks of life who are thoughtful and intelligent, and who embody the kind of spirit Andrew and Adam do. I'm delighted they've invited me to kibitz about their conversation.

In what follows I mention some tensions I've noticed in Andrew's and Adam's views in the hopes of enriching their already rich discussion, and suggest lines of development that they and their readers might have overlooked. I'll focus on the philosophical positions they stake out on mind and morals.

Adam says this:

> The mind *is* what the brain *does*. Rational thought, emotion, and consciousness arise from, and are produced by, the complex patterns of information that flow along the hundreds of trillions of neural connections in our heads.... Our scientific understanding of precisely *how* the brain produces the mind is in its very earliest stages.... Even so, we have abundant evidence that this view is true. We already know that all the functions of consciousness are produced by specific regions within the brain, and can be altered or lost when those brain regions are damaged or impaired.... Does this fit with a non-materialist theory of the self? If the mind is something more than the brain, how is it possible that a person can learn and grasp some new piece of information one moment, then have it completely slip from his consciousness the next?

These remarks are ambiguous among at least three different views:

1. Emergentism: thoughts and feelings are produced by states of the brain.
2. Psychophysical identity theory: thoughts and feelings are identical to states of the brain.
3. Functionalism: thoughts and feelings are identical to functional states, ones postulated by abstract descriptions that ignore a system's physical details and focus on what it does—in particular, how it correlates inputs with outputs.

Adam's claim that the brain produces the mind suggests some type of emergentism; his suggestion that the mind is nothing more than the brain suggests a psychophysical identity theory, and his claim that the mind is what the brain does suggests a commitment to functionalism. The difficulty is that these views are incompatible with each other. If the brain produces the mind, then it can't be identical to the mind since a thing can't produce itself. Likewise, if the mind is identical to the brain, then it is a concrete physical thing, not something posited by an abstract description whose states are merely approximated by those of a concrete physical thing. Given this crucial ambiguity, it's difficult to assess Adam's claim that "we have abundant evidence that this view is true," since it's not clear exactly what view he has in mind.

Foreword

Andrew, on the other hand, says that he leans "towards an Aristotelian-Thomistic hylomorphism." The trouble is that a hylomorphic account of thought, feeling, perception, and other mental phenomena is difficult to reconcile with Andrew's fondness for the view of consciousness defended by people like David Chalmers and Thomas Nagel. Many hylomorphists are repulsed by that kind of view since it is based on assumptions they reject.

Hylomorphism's basic idea is that some individuals, paradigmatically living things, consist of materials that are structured or organized in various ways. You and I are not mere quantities of physical materials; we are quantities of physical materials with a certain organization or structure. That structure is responsible for us being and persisting as humans, and it is responsible for us having the particular developmental, metabolic, reproductive, perceptive, and cognitive capacities we have. A simple example can help illustrate the hylomorphic notion of structure—call it *the squashing example*. Suppose we put Andrew in a strong bag—a very strong bag since we want to ensure that nothing leaks out when we squash him with several tons of force. Before squashing, the contents of the bag include one human being; after squashing, they include none. In addition, before squashing, the contents of the bag can think, feel, and act, but after they can't. What explains these differences in the contents of the bag pre- and post-squashing? The physical materials remain the same—none of them leaked out. What changed was instead the way those materials were organized or structured. That structure was responsible for there being a human before the squashing, and for that human having the capacities it had. Once that structure was destroyed, there no longer was a human with those capacities. Structure is thus a basic ontological principle: it concerns what things there are. It is also a basic explanatory principle: it concerns what things can do—the distinctive powers they have.

Now, the worldview that people like Chalmers and Nagel endorse—a worldview inherited from Descartes and other figures of the sixteenth and seventeenth centuries—claims that there is no such thing as form or structure in the hylomorphic sense. There is the world described by physics: a vast undifferentiated sea of matter and energy. And that world does not appear to have a place for consciousness. How is it possible, after all, for the movements of tiny particles to give rise to the rich qualitative conscious experiences we have? The difficulty of answering this question is the so-called hard problem of consciousness. But hylomorphists reject the assumptions on which the hard problem is based. From their perspective the problem can arise only for a worldview that rejects hylomorphic structure.

Hylomorphic structure carves out distinctive individuals from the otherwise undifferentiated sea of matter and energy described by our best physics, and it confers on those individuals distinctive powers. If hylomorphic structure exists, the physical universe is punctuated with pockets of organized change and stability—composite physical objects (paradigmatically living things) whose structures confer on them powers that distinguish what they can do from what unstructured materials can do. Those powers include the powers to think, feel, and perceive—manifestations of what philosophers like Chalmers and Nagel would call "consciousness." By contrast, a worldview that rejects hylomorphic structure lacks a basic principle to distinguish the parts of the physical universe that can think, feel, and perceive from those that can't, and without a basic principle that carves out zones with distinctive powers, the existence of those powers in the natural world can start to look inexplicable and mysterious. In a world without structure, there is nothing in the basic fabric of the universe that explains why Zone A has powers that Zone B lacks—nothing that explains why you, say, have the powers to think, feel, and perceive, while the materials surrounding you do not. If there is hylomorphic structure, however, the powers that you have to engage in conscious activities exist in the natural world simply because structure exists in the natural world. As a result, there is no hard problem of consciousness.

In addition, there no single thing called "consciousness" that cries out for explanation if hylomorphism is true. When we walk, talk, sing, dance, run, jump, and engage in the various other activities we do, we impose an order on the ways our parts operate. On the hylomorphic view, structured activities of this sort include thinking, feeling, and perceiving. When, for instance, I experience an emotion, I am engaging in an activity in which various parts of my nervous system and various objects in the environment operate in a coordinated way that unifies them into a single event. Just as I throw a baseball exactly if my parts and objects in the environment are coordinated throwing-a-baseball-wise, likewise I experience anger or enjoyment exactly if my parts and objects in the environment are coordinated anger- or enjoyment-wise. Conscious activities find a comfortable home in the natural world.

I've taken the time to describe the hylomorphic view because it offers a potential middle ground for Adam and Andrew. On the one hand, it implies that all of our powers are essentially embodied in the physiological mechanisms that compose us: we cannot engage in the activities we do apart from the coordinated operation of those mechanisms since our activities are composed of those operations. Just as it is impossible for me to throw a baseball unless my parts operate in the right coordinated way, the same is true of thinking, feeling, and perceiving. The hylomorphic view thus avoids positing nonphysical entities to explain psychological capacities—something Adam wants in a theory of mind.

On the other hand, the hylomorphic view implies that it is impossible to reduce explanations of thinking, feeling, and perceiving to explanations of physiological mechanisms. The reason is that there is more to these activities than the operation of those mechanisms; there is also the way the operations are coordinated or structured, and structure in general is something different from things that get structured. It is possible for parts of our nervous systems to be activated in the ways they are when, say, we are experiencing a particular emotion even though we are not experiencing the emotion in fact. Patients with pseudobulbar affect suddenly and unpredictably cry or laugh in ways that are indistinguishable from the ways they would if they were experiencing sadness or mirth, and yet they do not feel sad or amused. Parts of their nervous systems are activated in the ways they would be during a real emotional episode, and yet their activation fails to be coordinated in the way necessary to compose an emotion. The hylomorphic view is thus robustly antireductive despite its commitment to essential physical embodiment, and antireductionism is something that Andrew wants in a theory of mind. Perhaps, then, the hylomorphic view can give both Adam and Andrew what they want.

If we turn to morals, both Andrew and Adam express sympathy for a virtue ethical framework that takes human happiness or well-being to be central to moral evaluation. There are nevertheless two ways in which they might develop their respective views further. First, Adam says that he'd like for a moral framework to be based on a scientific understanding of human happiness and well-being. He nevertheless also says that he takes happiness to be a subjective experience—"a quale." If that's what happiness is, then there seems little hope of articulating a scientifically based moral framework since science works precisely by distancing itself from subjective appearances to achieve objectivity—a "view from nowhere," as Nagel calls it. In addition, if happiness is an irreducibly first-personal mental state, then it becomes unclear how it could be central to moral evaluation.

The reason is that our mental states needn't correspond either to our well-being or to general moral principles. We could be in a happy mental state while plugged into the Matrix, yet this wouldn't be human life at its best. Likewise, we could be in a happy mental state while doing morally horrific things. Unless Adam wants to embrace utilitarianism or some other hedonistic moral framework that reduces moral rightness to subjective feelings, it's not clear that his take on happiness really fits with the rest of his moral outlook.

Andrew, on the other hand, looks to ground his moral framework on God's goodness. He does not appear to endorse a divine command theory—a view according to which things are morally right exactly if they are commanded by God. He instead expresses sympathy for a virtue ethical framework like Aristotle's or Aquinas's. In that case, though, it's not clear why he insists on basing his moral framework on God. Aristotelian virtue ethics is based on the idea that biological beings like us can be in better or worse states, and that there are conditions that contribute to or detract from those states. A geranium in my garden can thrive or flourish only if it has the right soil, sunlight, and water. What makes something good or bad for the geranium is that it contributes to or detracts from the geranium's flourishing. Likewise, what makes something good or bad for humans is that it contributes to or detracts from our flourishing. Humans can flourish only if they cultivate the right kinds of conditions for themselves—including certain consistent ways of thinking, feeling, and acting, which Aristotle called virtues. For a moral framework along these lines to work, what's needed is an account of flourishing for members of our biological kind, and an account of what sorts of things contribute to or detract from it. It's not evident to what extent theological considerations are necessary for accomplishing this task. Perhaps there is an argument to the effect that an account of human flourishing cannot be given apart from an appeal to God's goodness, but we have yet to hear an argument of that sort.

The foregoing remarks point toward another way in which Adam's and Andrew's views might converge. Each of their views is committed to claims that are sticking points for the other. The Aristotelian framework I've just outlined represents an alternative to both that depends neither on a subjective characterization of happiness, nor on an appeal to God's goodness as a ground for moral judgment. It might thus offer them a framework for moral evaluation that is mutually acceptable.

Foreword

There's much more I could say about Adam's and Andrew's conversation, but I hope I've said enough to contribute in a small way to their ongoing effort to live the examined life.

William Jaworski
Associate Professor of Philosophy
Fordham University

Introduction

While there has been a great deal of public debate about belief in God in recent years (much of it a little petulant, much of it positively ferocious), the concept of God around which the arguments have run their seemingly interminable courses has remained strangely obscure the whole time. The more scrutiny one accords these debates, moreover, the more evident it becomes that often the contending parties are not even talking about the same thing; and I would go as far as to say that on most occasions none of them is talking about God in any coherent sense at all.[1]

—DAVID BENTLEY HART, *THE EXPERIENCE OF GOD*

The Greek prefix μετά, or *Meta*, is an interesting one. The literal translation means "after," "beside," or "among," though it's used frequently as a description for "about" or "beyond." Depending upon the word it's prefixed, the word in its entirety can take on a curious meaning. Take the word "metadiscussion," for example. Bill O'Reilly and Bill Maher screaming at each other over the Affordable Care Act is *not* a metadiscussion. A metadiscussion is a discussion *about* a discussion—in this case a discussion on what the Affordable Care Act is *about* (the matter at hand, presentation of opposing viewpoints, etc.).

Now consider the word *metaphysics*, what Aristotle described as "first philosophy". If physics involves the study of matter, metaphysics considers the ultimate nature of existence *beyond* matter or *beyond* empirical validation. The finitude of time, the existence of God, the nature of consciousness, the foundations for morality—a scientist may claim "the universe is infinite," "God obviously exists," or "morality is completely subjective"—or

---

1. Hart, *The Experience of God*, 1.

Introduction

utter many other similar statements. In doing so, however, she speaks not as a scientist, but as a metaphysician.

I don't know how it happened, but I fell in love with philosophy. It's tempting to say that it was sparked by my study of science and engineering, though such a description would be mistaken. True, coming off eighteen years of theological and political spoon-feeding, my comrades and I were released into the dangerous ideological battlefield we call higher learning. True, in the embrace of ideological potpourri, many of us were afforded, for the first time, an opportunity to seek truth with an open mind. Thinkers, seekers, explorers—we would finally embrace the opportunity afforded.

Not exactly. Many just embraced the beliefs of their youth. Many just ran to the opposite side of the spectrum. Many just chose what was fashionable or preferable. Few, including myself, were willing to take Descartes's challenge:

> That in order to seek truth, it is necessary once in the course of our life, to doubt, as far as possible, of all things. As we were at one time children, and as we formed various judgments regarding the objects presented to our senses, when as yet we had not the entire use of our reason, numerous prejudices stand in the way of our arriving at the knowledge of truth; and of these it seems impossible for us to rid ourselves, unless we undertake, once in our lifetime, to doubt of all those things in which we may discover even the smallest suspicion of uncertainty.[2]

Looking back, it's unsurprising. In my experience, only the few are interested in sincerely exploring the big questions. Many are annoyed at even a gentle push against their worldview, perhaps no more prevalent on the topic of God. For many of the religious complexion, God obviously exists; for many of the irreligious, God obviously doesn't.

My theological "skepticism" was not a result of genuine inquiry and skepticism, but of genuine *disinterest*. *True* skeptics have the courage to take Descartes's challenge, to doubt all views, including their own. Mine was simply a position of indifference and I was not alone. In hindsight, this was not necessarily a bad thing. Perhaps I thought I was ready, but ran out of gas along the way. I may have just returned to the traditions of my youth and the dogmatic beyond. That, or perhaps I went in the opposite direction, running as far as I could into the new land. Wherever I would have ended up, if I was not truly ready, it would have been in vain, should I have

---

2. Descartes, *Principles of Philosophy*, 130.

Introduction

prematurely accepted Descartes's challenge, yet not heeded Kierkegaard's warning: "the crowd is untruth."[3]

It's not just the destination, it's also the journey. There are many lands and many tribes and it's readily apparent how many are chained to various ideologies. To the challenge of Descartes's, and the warning of Kierkegaard, add the allegory of Plato's cave:

> Imagine human beings living in an underground, cavelike dwelling. . . . They've been there since childhood, fixed in the same place, with their necks and legs fettered, able to see only in front of them, because their bonds prevent them from turning their heads around. Light is provided by a fire burning far above and behind them. . . . They're like us. Do you suppose, first of all, that these prisoners see anything of themselves and one another besides the shadows that the fire casts on the wall in front of them?[4]

Chained by bias and indifference, how could I really seek truth? Quite simply, I didn't. It would only be years later when a spirit of willingness would awake the philosopher within me. Prior to that, I never cared enough to really seek. Living with the crowd in the shadows comes with many benefits. Cutting through the chains and thinking deeply and openly about the big questions is an exhausting undertaking that comes with many risks. As a skeptical biomedical engineer approaching the intersection of faith and reason, I was afraid what I might find.

It would be a serious undertaking, one I chronicled in my book *Proof of Divine*. The aim would be no less than the absolute proof of God's existence. Perhaps I overshot things a bit, though the endeavor was far from in vain. While I failed in reaching my destination, I found myself along the way. Two significant changes would unfold. First, I reached *faith* in a radical new way: it became my own. Secondly, my destination changed. It became less about proof and more about justified belief and having a conversation. What do we believe and why? Growing increasingly interested in the conversation on God's existence, so too would follow many of the other big questions. In this marked the ultimate awaking of my inner philosopher—a decision to seek, and seek deeply, with an open mind, and to follow the truth wherever it leads. Philosophy, after all, is Greek for "love of wisdom."

---

3. Kierkegaard, "On the Dedication to 'That Single Individual.'"
4. Plato, *The Republic,* Book VII, 186–87.

Introduction

I'm now interested in a brave metadiscussion, not a petty discussion. The challenge is that petty discussion on these matters seems to be the road most travelled. I'd like to get off the interstate. As the spirit of meta implies "about" or "beyond," so too will be the twofold purpose of the project:

1. *About*—on God, the big questions, and the just city, what are some of the matters at hand? Why do we believe what we believe? What are the opposing views?

2. *Beyond*—what does a meaningful discussion look like? *Beyond* the typical academic debates, *beyond* the dogmatism of the opposing sides, *beyond* the typical *ad hominem* attacks.

The aim of this book is to explore these matters with someone that is interested in having a *genuine* discussion. Someone with the maturity to be passionate with principle, yet respectful in discourse. Someone with the courage to reflect on the *matter at hand*, not just *their hand in the matter*. Someone in a similar place in life, a young working professional and author with an interest in theology, philosophy, science, politics, and culture—a brave truth seeker that ended up in an entirely different place. I would not have to look far.

After I published my first book, I began blogging at *Patheos* in the Christian circles. As I settled into my own blog, I would visit some of my neighbors in the atheist circles to learn more about their perspectives. It did not take long for Adam Lee to catch my eye. Many bloggers have very specific interests (and rarely get off topic) and few have interest in talking *to* people with opposing views (though they certainly like to talk *about* people with opposing views). Adam's topics were varied and his perspectives on philosophy, theology, and culture were eloquent and thought-provoking. We certainly had different perspectives, but I know intelligence and swagger when I see it. His blog, *Daylight Atheism*, later the title of his book, also caught my attention. In his statement of principles,[5] Adam describes himself as an atheist and materialist and cites a timeless line from the famous Greek materialist philosopher Democritus: "by convention sweet is sweet, bitter is bitter, hot is hot, cold is cold, color is color; but in truth there are only atoms and the void." He espouses secular humanism and universal utilitarianism as his moral philosophy and maintains that morality is objective. Politically, he describes himself as a classical liberal and has a skeptical optimism for the future. He sees atheism as a beautiful and inspiring world-

---

5. Lee, "Statement of Principles," Patheos.com

Introduction

view and "force for good."[6] This, I remember thinking to myself, could be interesting. What follows is our uncommon exchange turned friendship.

Andrew Murtagh

---

6. Lee, "Why Atheism is a Force for Good," Patheos.com

ROUND 1

Opening Statements

Nacho: How come you have never been baptized?
Esqueleto: Because, I never got around to it ok? I don't know why you always have to be judging me, because I only believe in science.

—NACHO LIBRE

Adam,

Thank you again for collaborating with me on this immensely important project. Like you, I am a fellow enthusiast of free thought, a spirit I've found lacking in the matters in which we are about to embark. I share in the uncanny notion that we can change the world, one idea at a time, one person at a time. I think it all starts with a spark, free thought, and creativity—from there the inspiration and motivation to see it through. It is truly an honor to work with you towards this endeavor of an uncommon exchange.

If we stay true to the goals of the project, we'll get to the heart of some of the big questions. I'm very interested in learning more about your views. If the feeling is mutual, what follows will extend far beyond the typical production—arrogant and *ad hominem* in nature. The same old dogmatic and disrespectful discord is far from *edifying*. Where are the *true* freethinkers who love the debate and discussion? Where are the clear and concise opinions and relevant discussions of the current day? The matters at hand and our respective views—let's challenge each other to contrasting viewpoints and apply those concepts to real-world issues.

META

On that note, let us commence! I briefly summarized your statement of principles in the introduction, so I'll start by laying out my own. My background is in biomedical engineering and my day job is in the medical device industry where I've worked in engineering, sales, and management. In my free time, which there never seems to be enough of lately, I study philosophy. My specific interests lie in metaphysics, philosophy of religion, and philosophy of mind—why anything exists at all, the problem of change and knowledge, morality, consciousness—the big questions. My thesis is that every worldview is deeply religious and speculative. Though we cling to a rational foundation, we all have a "leap of faith." In regards to my specific Christian worldview, I embrace the religious tenets as speaking to the heart of the human condition, revealing a God worth loving. More on that later.

To contrast your statement of principles with mine, I'll give a brief overview, which I'm sure we'll expand upon through the duration of the book. Ontologically, I'm a realist (there are mind-independent truths). God's existence, moral truth, mathematical truth, scientific truth—mark me down as a realist.

Metaphysically, I'm drawn to Aristotelian-Thomistic metaphysics, which is distinct from dualism and materialism, frustrating and confusing many of my friendly theistic and atheistic interlocutors. Theologically, I consider myself a "Nicene Catholic" (this is not a movement, but a self-description to describe both my faith journey and current perspective). I was raised Catholic from my father's side, my mother's side is Greek Orthodox, and my wife Naomi's side is Protestant. Naomi was raised Protestant and later converted to Catholicism. I would go on to protest both the Catholic Church and God's existence for several reasons (I'm sure we can relate on much here), and now associate as both Catholic and Christian— ecumenical in attitude, affirming the Nicene Creed with all Christians and Catholics, though I definitely swing Catholic in philosophical theology (classical theism and scholastic metaphysics). Politically, I'm an independent, though even that label bothers me. In terms of my outlook for the future, we both share, in your words, a "skeptical optimism."

All that said, we have much to discuss! Perhaps an appropriate starting point for our discussion and your reply would be clarifying your views on morality and secular humanism, not just practically, but metaphysically. I've always been intrigued at this topic as many theists and atheists claim the consequence of atheism is moral skepticism/irrealism. You and I are both moral realists and see morality as objective. Are your views in line with Sam Harris's in *The Moral Landscape*—defining morality as the science of human "well-being"? As an atheist, how do you arrive at morality being objective?

META

And I won't breathe the bracing air when I'm gone
And I can't even worry 'bout my cares when I'm gone
Won't be asked to do my share when I'm gone
So I guess I'll have to do it while I'm here

—PHIL OCHS, "WHEN I'M GONE"

Andrew,

When I got your initial letter, I wondered at first who this stranger was and why he'd taken the time to write to me of all people. But the more I read, the more I realized that this dialogue was just the kind of project that I'd be interested in.

I admit, when I see two people shouting at each other on TV, my first impulse is to change the channel. I find that those kinds of "debates" generate a lot of spectacle, but little illumination. Too much anger and vitriol, like fire raging out of control, fills up the room with smoke that quickly obscures whatever was being debated in the first place.

At the same time, I continue to believe that a friendly debate between two very different viewpoints is the best way to find out where the truth lies. You can always count on someone coming from a different background to probe at the weak spots in your philosophy, the parts that are all too easy to gloss over when you're only talking to the like-minded. Truth is best revealed in the light of the sparks that fly when two worldviews bump up against each other, illuminating the corners where they mesh and the rough areas where they clash. And that's all the more true when it comes to religion and atheism. These are the deepest and most fascinating questions there are, which makes them inherently interesting. Who among us hasn't pondered what this strange existence really means and how it came to be?

You laid out your background, so here's a little about mine. As you of course know, I'm an atheist, which means I don't believe in anything beyond or above the physical world. Everything that exists consists of matter and energy interacting in the arena of space and time in accordance with the overarching principles which we call natural laws. I believe that reality exists and is knowable through empirical observation and the exercise of reason. I also consider myself a humanist, which means I believe that human beings are the wellsprings of ultimate value and that our wants and well-being should be treated as paramount. My day job is in software engineering, but like you, I've always been drawn to these bigger questions.

You asked about my views on morality, and that's a good starting point, because that's really what it all comes down to. No matter what we think of someone else's beliefs or customs, however strange we may think them, the most important question is whether we can share the same planet together.

My answer is that morality is the science of human happiness. In the same way that medicine is the science of restoring the body to health (whatever your definition of "health" is), I contend that morality is the same thing, but with a broader purpose: not just fixing what's gone wrong, but figuring out how we should treat each other so that all our lives contain the most happiness (whatever your definition of "happiness" is).

I'm not saying that there's a provable answer to the question of what we should do in every possible moral dilemma. But I am saying that we can know, and can prove to a reasonable person's satisfaction, that some principles work better than others, and that we should construct our society along those lines so as to make it a better place for everyone. This is similar to what Sam Harris said in his book *The Moral Landscape*, although I flatter myself that I've been thinking independently along these lines for quite a while. I wrote an essay expounding similar views in 2001![1]

My contention is that morality should be based not on armchair reasoning or religious decree, but on evidence: the empirical observation of the world which shows that some things are more conducive to happiness and well-being than others. Once you accept this idea, the consequence of morality being an objective truth falls out of that, in the same way that the answer to any other scientific question is objective. That's not to say it will always be easy to discover, but if morality seems vague or subjective, it's only because we're asking such big, complicated questions, and our evidence is still so incomplete.

I think that most people, including most atheists, who say they're moral relativists really mean that they don't grant any single book, tradition, or authority figure the sole right to decide what's right or wrong; that they find good ideas in many different viewpoints. And I agree with that! I doubt that anyone, including me, has the full picture of what's moral and what isn't. My most important objective isn't to defend a specific set of moral principles as established truth—although obviously I do argue for certain conclusions—but to get people to think about morality in the right way, to

---

1. Lee, Adam. "The Ineffable Carrot and the Infinite Stick." Patheos.com.

ask the right questions. Once we're doing that, I think we'll converge on the same answers without too much fuss. More to the point, I think humanity has been doing that for a long time. That's what Steven Pinker points out, in his book *The Better Angels of Our Nature*, about the "rights revolutions" that have swept the globe over the past several centuries.[2] Democracy, universal suffrage, women's rights, the abolition of slavery, animal rights, and other moral ideas that once seemed shockingly radical have all become widely accepted and uncontroversial.

    I find that the greatest source of opposition to this progress is the view that someone—some perfect source—has already told us what morality is, and all we have to do is find where it's written down. I would argue that this idea is unworkable for discovering moral truth just as it's unworkable for discovering scientific truth. So here's my question to you: To what extent do you think we can derive morality from religious belief? Do you believe that the Bible and other religious texts are trustworthy guides to how we should live, or do they need to be taken with a grain of salt? And whatever your answer, what do you think the best way is to communicate that message to everyone else?

---

2. Pinker, *The Better Angels of Our Nature*

ROUND 2

Faith, Reason, and Morality, Part I

Carter: The stars . . . really one of God's good ones.
Edward: So you think a being of some sort did all this?
Carter: You don't?
Edward: . . . No.
Carter: It's called faith.
Edward: I honestly envy people who have faith, I just can't get my head around it.
Carter: Maybe your head's in the way.
Edward: Carter, we've all had hundreds of these discussions and everyone of them always hits the same wall. . . . And nobody has ever gotten over that wall. . . . We live, we die, and the wheels on the bus go round and round. . . . You're not claiming you know something I don't?
Carter: No, I just have faith.
Edward: Hallelujah brother, now pass the mustard.

—THE BUCKET LIST

Adam,

Before we proceed, I wanted to tell you how much I enjoyed our "debate" at the Midtown Scholar in Harrisburg. Even though we had an official moderator and disagreed on many issues, the entire afternoon felt more like hanging out with an old friend. The debate, getting to know you personally, introducing you to my friends and family, the "post-debate party," and then spending the evening with you was truly a pleasure. On that note, let's proceed!

As I said at our debate, I feel we are both passionate truth seekers and that you are in good company as I'm a fellow skeptic and self-proclaimed "doubting theist." As someone who believes that critical inquiry and skepticism is paramount to seeking truth, doubt is an essential component. From go, know that I am more than empathetic to Richard Dawkins's challenge that "we are all atheists about most of the gods that humanity has ever believed in. Some of us just go one god further."[1] I am an atheist for every other god. I can't get past *God* and Christianity specifically, which I'm sure we'll be discussing further. Nevertheless, I'm enthused that we share kindred spirits on the commitment to follow the truth wherever it leads.

Obviously, we've arrived at different endpoints with theism. For me, God is the end of philosophical reasoning—from physics to metaphysics, contingent to Necessary, being to Being, good to Goodness. Existence, causation, love, universal truths, consciousness—the seemingly metaphysical nature of being puts us both in the precarious situation of trying to account for these dimensions of human experience. As I stated earlier, I ultimately feel every worldview is religious and speculative, having both physical and metaphysical components; the physical *empirically validated* and the metaphysical *philosophically speculated*. With morality, for example, we're both realists and place immense value on empirical validation, though we differ on the metaphysical accounting. But we're all metaphysicians. It's inescapable.

This would begin to address your question on "what extent we can derive morality from religious belief." If the religious belief had no rational foundation, *none* would be my answer. If the belief was simply a "perfect source" that "tells us what morality is" and that we just need to "find where it is written down"—why would I feel compelled to accept that? Such a belief would be simple fideism (the view that faith is independent of reason). The Latin and Greek translations for faith are "trust." As a truth seeker, I believe trust should only be given from a rational foundation.

Certainly, faith involves subjectivity and a dimension of knowledge that extends beyond reason. On the former, I'll happily admit that a Kierkegaardian leap of faith plays a necessary role towards a passionate and subjective faith commitment. On the latter, I'll also assert that the experience of God and trusting Jesus as the revelation of God ultimately surpasses

---

1. Dawkins, *A Devil's Chaplain*, 150.

reason. Nevertheless, Christianity requires *first the rationality of theism*. Only thereafter is "faith" justified. Why would one even consider Christianity if there was not a strong metaphysical foundation for the existence of God to begin with? Same with the historical foundations, why consider Christianity if Jesus never existed? For my faith and trust, reason is the bedrock. In the words of Aquinas,

> The existence of God and other like truths about God, which can be known by natural reason, are not articles of faith, but are preambles to the articles; for faith presupposes natural knowledge.[2]

Though faith ultimately "surpasses the capacity of reason," truth is truth and "truth that the human reason is naturally endowed to know cannot be opposed to the truth of the Christian faith."[3] In this view, reason and faith are not opposed, just different dimensions of knowledge. But make no mistake, for philosophical theists, reason is the bedrock of theism. Reasoned metaphysical propositions (theism/naturalism or moral realism/non-realism) ultimately hinge upon a reasoned metaphysical foundation (the ultimate nature of existence, the problem of universals, the problem of change, the problem of knowledge, etc.).

Back to your question, one doesn't need the Bible to have a sense of morality or God. Philosophical arguments for the existence of God don't touch the Bible. The history of philosophy itself was about challenging religious superstition in contemplating the nature of existence. Such reasoning equally challenged bad naturalistic ideas (change is an illusion) and bad theistic ideas (polytheism). For philosophical theists, the "God of the Philosophers" is posited only after the nature of being is considered. Why does anything exist? Is nature eternal and self-caused? What are physical substances? Are there universals? If so, how can we have knowledge of them? These questions lie at the heart of metaphysics and were the endeavor of the ancient Greeks in philosophizing. Some timeless metaphysical theories arose for reasoned answers to these questions; naturalism and dualism the most prevalent to date. As I mentioned earlier, I'm immensely attracted to the metaphysics of Aristotle, which is distinct from dualism and naturalism, though it combines some key elements of both theories.

At one end, I understand the appeal of naturalism. Parmenides was a materialist famous for the idea of *nihil fit ex nihilo* ("nothing comes from

---

2. Aquinas, ST, Ia, q. 2, a. 2.
3. Aquinas, *Contra Gentiles*.

nothing"). Where that showed promise, combining that doctrine with his materialism, he moved that matter must be eternal, indestructible, and unchanged—that change is an illusion and knowledge is possible through the intellection of unchangeable matter. Good start, but rocky finish. Another naturalist would have to carry the torch. Enter Democritus, who you know well, who agreed with Parmenides that "out of nothing, nothing comes" and that matter must be eternal; yet denied that change is an illusion. Democritus reasoned that knowledge of matter and motion will account for everything.

At the other end, I understand the appeal of dualism. Plato rejected Parmenides's materialism and illusion of change. Instead, he maintained that the sensible world is full of change, and knowledge is possible through the immaterial realm of unchanging, timeless, eternal Forms, grasped only by the intellect. Universal truths such as mathematics and morality are secure and the intellect, the rationally free conscious self, is timeless, having access to these timeless truths. Plato's dualism is so strong conceptually that it still resonates with theists and atheists alike. It solves several philosophical problems, though it creates other ones with the "far-out-ness" of the theory.

Enter Aristotle's hylomorphism, as William Jaworksi notes, "a compound of the Greek words *hyle* and *morphe*," which is the view that things "consist of both matter and form."[4] Aristotle agreed with his teacher Plato that there are forms, but they're *in* nature, not in a separate immaterial realm. Reality, in Aristotle's view, is an irreducible composite of material (matter) and form (immaterial ontology). Ontology is now in nature, but it hinges on the concept of being and causation. Aristotle agreed with Parmenides that "out of nothing, nothing comes" but rejected his view that change is an illusion. Aristotle, in accounting for change, brilliantly divided up being into potentiality and actuality. Now, something doesn't come into being from nonbeing, it's actualized from a state of potential being.

I find Aristotle's metaphysics irresistible for such a balanced overview of change, knowledge, and being. Common sense, science, and reason all have a celebrated portion in the truth-seeking endeavor. Material change is obvious and things in nature exist in between a state of potentiality and actuality. Though material change is undeniable, knowledge is still possible *from this world*. Our senses can certainly deceive us, but they are the starting point to knowledge. From our senses, scientific and rational deliberation

---

4. Jaworski, *Philosophy of Mind*, 270.

can be applied to reach objective truths. In other words, knowledge of universal truths is abstracted from our senses. Regarded as the founder of logic and the scientific method, he was a true empiricist and ontological realist. Matter and motion alone, he felt, were explanatorily insufficient. It seems there are final and formal causes in nature. From this flows teleology, the idea that there are intrinsic ends, purposes, or goals in all existent things that can be actualized from a certain potential, given its nature.

Only after a reasoned philosophy of nature (which I maintain is hylomorphic and teleological) can one rationally maintain metaphysical truths (such as theism and moral realism). Being (potency/act), causation, change, and goodness—these seem like real features of reality. Because anything exists at all, because there are ends in nature, because there is such thing as objective goodness, we *reason* towards a Final Cause, "Pure Act," Being and Goodness Itself, the Necessity of which all contingent things depend. God, pure actuality, has breathed potentiality, motion, and goodness into nature—a nature that has cultivated rational, moral, and free creatures.

All this goes back to your original question on deriving morality from religious belief. To me, the deeper question is the following: *To what extent can we derive objective morality from any system of metaphysics?* We can't unless that view provides moral ontology. No moral philosophy should be taken seriously unless it rests upon a coherent and consistent system of metaphysics. Why does anything exist? What is the good, the true, and the beautiful? Do they exist objectively? What is knowledge? What is the conscious self? Are we rationally free creatures? Again, we're all metaphysicians. From the view of our critics, we both stand accused as religious—me for God as the reasoned end of Truth, Goodness, and Beauty (Being itself)—and you for matter itself as the reasoned end of being, truth, goodness, and beauty.

Before we get too deep into morality, though, I would love your thoughts on the reason and faith distinction. You're an atheist, so you obviously haven't been compelled by these arguments. But do you feel that most people (believers and skeptics) approach the question of God's existence in a similar way?

META

We must remember that most men have been controlled by their surroundings. Most of the intelligent men in Turkey are followers of Mahomet. They were rocked in the cradle of the Koran, they received their religious opinions as they did their features—from their parents. . . . The same may be said of the Christians of our country. Their belief is the result, not of thought, of investigation, but of surroundings.[5]

—ROBERT GREEN INGERSOLL, *"WHICH WAY?"* (1884)

Andrew,

Thanks again for your fairness and you and your family's hospitality at the Midtown Scholar debate. It was a pleasure, in spite of the sudden and terrible blizzard that stranded me in town overnight! As I said in my first letter, I enjoy participating in debates that are more about a friendly quest for the truth, rather than a dramatic quest for ratings, and I think ours met that standard. Having a scrupulously fair moderator helped as well—and believe me, I've been in debates that had biased moderators, and you can tell the difference.

To answer your question, I think that believers and skeptics tend to approach the question of God's existence in different ways. As you say, religious skeptics like myself treat this as an empirical question. We investigate the evidence, find it insufficient to support a commitment, and therefore withhold belief. This is particularly true of the classical philosophical and metaphysical arguments for God's existence, which either assume what they want to prove or hold forth conclusions that simply don't follow from their premises.

Very few, if any, theists come at this question in the same way. That would mean investigating all the world's religious traditions, weighing the evidence for and against each one of them, and ultimately deciding that the facts are sufficient to support one particular conception of God while ruling out the others. I don't think I've ever met a person who can credibly claim to have done that.

You wrote about the contrasting approaches of faith versus reason and how these both play a part in leading you to the theological position you

---

5. Ingersoll, *The Works of Robert G. Ingersoll*, 438.

now occupy. However, there's another possibility you paid less attention to, perhaps because it's less relevant in your specific case, but I'd go so far as to say it's by far the most common way that people all over the world come to believe in a certain religion. That's the route of tradition.

What I mean by this is that most people believe in God because it's the belief held by most people in their cultural in-group, the one that defines their identity and differentiates them from outsiders, and it's safest and easiest to go with the flow. In harsher societies this is backed up by ostracism, harassment, or even severe legal punishments for nonbelievers and dissenters, but it's not usually enforced in such a draconian manner. More often, it's simply passed down as received wisdom, what everyone in our society knows, what makes us who we are, and children and young people are taught that holding these beliefs is the way to show proper respect to your family, your ancestors, and your culture. When a belief is woven into the fabric of the culture like that, few people will even think to question it.

Obviously, most people are taught a certain set of religious beliefs as unquestioned truth from childhood, and that's the major way that every tradition perpetuates itself. But even if you're not indoctrinated in childhood, it's also the case that people who go through an existential crisis and convert later in life will tend to pick the religion that's most common in their culture and social circles, just because it's the one they're most familiar with and have the most chance to encounter. (I once read a book by a pastor named Dave Schmelzer, who related the story of how he came to be converted to Christianity: he was lost on a late-night drive and came across two large, floodlit crosses in a row, which he attributes to divine providence.[6] Well, what other large religious symbols was he expecting to see in the United States of America? If he'd encountered two mosques in a row, that would have been much more unusual.)

You mentioned faith and reason as complementary approaches, but I think that in an irreducible sense, these two contradict each other. If God's existence, nature, or desires could be determined solely by reason, no faith would be required. Since faith is required, that forecloses the possibility that God's existence is a conclusion derived from studying the evidence. The opposite holds true as well, of course: if God's existence is a conclusion grounded in evidence, then it must be the case that evidence could disprove it, which is a possibility I've almost never heard a religious person willing to grant.

6. Schmelzer, *Not the Religious Type.*

This is where tradition and culture come into the picture. If belief in God was purely a leap of faith, an unquestioning step beyond what reason can prove or justify, then choosing a set of religious beliefs ought to be as random a process as picking numbers out of a hat. Obviously, that's not what happens. Religions rise to dominance at certain places and times, thrive for a while, then mutate into new forms or fade away as they're replaced by different beliefs. Just by knowing where and when someone was born, you can predict with high confidence what beliefs they'll hold, and that would only be true if the acquisition of religious belief was culturally influenced.

You suggested that naturalism is equally arbitrary, but I wouldn't agree with that. The great advantage of naturalism is that it asks us to believe only in things that can be measured, observed, and objectively experienced—the tests that anyone can carry out for themselves, with results that everyone will get as long as they follow the same procedure. It doesn't ask us to believe extraordinary claims without extraordinary evidence, to accept mysteries solely because they're mysteries, or to infer anything about physical reality from subjective, internal mental states.

And again, I'd point out, the proof is that there are no competing cultural traditions in science, the way there are in religion. Scientists from different cultures can and readily do come to the same conclusions about what does and doesn't exist in the world, and when scientific debates do arise, they persist only until they're settled by some new evidence or definitive test. Imagine if scientists were still arguing about whether everything is made of the four classical elements, or whether disease is transmitted by invisible sickness-causing miasmas, or whether light is a wave in the rarefied medium of the luminiferous ether. Yet that's exactly the situation that the world's religions find themselves in even after centuries of disputation: still divided by the same theological differences with no prospect of reconciliation.

The key ingredient that science has and religion mostly doesn't is doubt, which is why I was intrigued by your self-identification as a doubting theist. That was striking, since doubt isn't treated as an essential element, or is even shunned as positively harmful, in most forms of Christianity, whereas you seem to place it front and center. That's a welcome and necessary corrective to the harms done in the name of religion, which usually flow from excessive certainty.

Even so, I wonder how far your doubt takes you. You said that you "can't get past" Christianity, but why do you think that is? If belief is a leap of faith that surpasses the capacity of reason, what is it that drove you to this particular leap, rather than any of the other countless ones that were open to you? Why believe God was incarnated in the person of Jesus Christ, rather than, say, believing that God expressed his will for humanity in a perfect Arabic document called the Qur'an which was given to the final prophet Mohammed? Or why not believe that God is a cosmic being named Brahma who created himself out of a lotus flower which sprouted from the navel of Vishnu?

This is where I think the route of tradition comes in. If you were born in Mecca, that Kierkegaardian leap into the absurd would very likely have landed you in Islam instead. In Kolkata, it might instead have taken you to Hinduism. Wherever and whenever a person is born, it's almost always the dominant religion that seems the most normal, the most natural, the most appealing to them. However you personally came to hold your faith, do you think it's a coincidence that you're a Christian in a time and place where Christianity is dominant?

ROUND 3

Faith, Reason, and Morality, Part II

Where a man's metaphysics comes to an end, his religion begins. But the only path which can lead him to the point where true religion begins must of necessity lead him beyond the contemplation of essences, up to the very mystery of existence. This path is not very hard to find, but few are those who dare to follow it to the end.[1]

—ETIENNE GILSON, *GOD AND PHILOSOPHY*

Adam,

I thoroughly enjoyed our radio debate on the Nick Givas Program on the Fairfield University airwaves! Thanks for your feedback on faith, reason, and tradition. I think it brings up an important distinction between metaphysical truth (ontology) and knowledge of such an assertions (epistemology). For the sake of argument, let's take my previous definition of knowledge to be "justified true belief." It sounds as if we both agree that one's metaphysical view is a destination, while epistemology (reason, empiricism, etc.) is a route, method, and justification of that worldview.

To your question on tradition, am I surprised that I am a Christian in a Christian nation? *No.* Am I surprised that person "X" is an atheist in an atheist nation? *No.* Am I surprised that person "Y" is a Hindu in a Hindu nation? *No.* As a truth seeker, I'm equally unimpressed with any view that is founded solely on tradition as it says nothing of the truth of that view.

---

1. Gilson, *God and Philosophy*, 148.

Perhaps most raised atheist remain atheists, most raised Lutheran remain Lutheran, and most raised Hindu remain Hindu. Worldview by tradition just speaks to the sheepish human condition, as Kierkegaard called "the Christendom" and Nietzsche called "the herd."

We agree that tradition is not a reliable epistemology. To me this is apparent not only in religion, but politics, or any philosophy. One's philosophical views, if they wish to be reasonable, should be justified. As someone who values reason, I've spared neither theism (all forms) nor naturalism (or any ideal) from skepticism and critical inquiry. I am empathetic to atheism as I've enjoyed its utility. As I said earlier, I'm an atheist for every other god, yet have not been able to look past *God* and Christianity. We'll get to Christianity in detail, but it all starts with a generic foundation that is not specific to Christianity: philosophical theism.

You mentioned that you treat the God question as "empirical." With the lack of empirical evidence, you withhold belief. You also touched upon the nature of science, scientific debate, and how it's an entirely different situation with theology. With that, you find the metaphysical arguments for God's existence "either assume what they want to prove or hold forth conclusions that simply don't follow from their premises."

As an empiricist, philosopher, and metaphysical realist, I would of course point out the difference between empirical knowledge (science) and philosophical knowledge (reason). Science, as you mentioned, is about verifying facts about the natural world. Looking for God empirically (under a rock, hiding in the clouds, or in background noise) is doomed for failure as the case for God presented is a philosophical/metaphysical one. I would also point out that debates happen all the time in science; not on what is seen under the microscope, but the overall philosophical interpretation. The various interpretations of quantum mechanics or cosmology (Big Bang, Multiverse, etc.) would just be a few examples. As I mentioned in the introduction, the physicist claiming that "the universe is infinite" is doing so philosophically. Such will always be the case—whenever philosophical interpretations are up for grabs, there will always be discord. Consequently, theologians and philosophers will always debate, as this is the nature of this form of knowledge. You're a moral realist. Shall we throw out moral realism because philosophers continue to debate the nature of morality? Science is science. Philosophy is philosophy. My case for God is a philosophical one, so I would also of course take issue that metaphysical arguments simply presuppose their conclusions or that their conclusions don't follow their premises. Following the thought of Aristotle and Aquinas, I see God as the reasoned *end* of metaphysical realism—from the contingent to the necessary, particulars to universals, matter and motion to formal and final causes—the Unmoved Mover. Because anything exists at all, because objective goodness exists—there must be Being and Goodness Itself—a Transcendent Cause.

You mentioned that "if God's existence, nature, or desires could be determined solely by reason, no faith would be required." Many thinkers may agree on reason being sufficient to arrive at God's existence (though I think many would take issue with our having *complete* knowledge of God's nature—and rightly so). But let's stick with reason being sufficient for *some* knowledge of God. Take Voltaire, for example. He was a deist who felt that God's existence is self-evident, not requiring any element of faith: "What is faith? Is it to believe that which is evident? No. It is perfectly evident to my mind that there exists a necessary, eternal, supreme, and intelligent being. This is no matter of faith, but of reason."[2] Einstein believed in an impersonal God "who reveals Himself in the lawful harmony of the world, not in a God who concerns Himself with the fate and the doings of mankind."[3] Philosopher Anthony Flew's conversion from atheism to an impersonal theism was due solely to his "pilgrimage of reason" and a "renewed study of the classical philosophical arguments."[4] If these thinkers are right, reason is all that's needed for some knowledge of God (and you should ditch your atheism).

What I find curious is your point on knowledge of God's existence, nature, and desires "solely by reason" and your conclusion "since faith is required, that forecloses the possibility that God's existence is a conclusion derived from studying the evidence." Why all or none? This rejects the very possibility that we can have some finite knowledge of God.

On my Kierkegaardian interest in Christianity, allow me to clarify. I find the rational tenets of Christianity compelling, but they can only take one so far. The faith dimension, the first-person experience of God, the subjective, passionate, and existential leap of faith, and spiritual transformation in Christ—this is the *being* of a Christian. In keeping with Kierkegaard,

> What use would it be to be able to propound the meaning of Christianity, to explain many separate facts, if it had no deeper meaning

2. Voltaire, *Philosophical Dictionary*.
3. Isaacson, *Einstein*, 388–89.
4. Flew, *There is a God*, 88–89.

for me and for my life? Certainly I won't deny that I still accept an imperative of knowledge, and that one can also be influenced by it, but then it must be taken up alive in me, and this is what I now see as the main point.[5]

As I said earlier, for the truth seeker, fideism is unacceptable so we'll agree that prescribing to *any* belief while closing your mind to reason and empiricism is just simple fanaticism. Of course, reason and empiricism should guide any worldview. The existential Kierkegaardian perspective, however, reminds us that reason and empiricism, within themselves, are deficient in making a subjective and passionate worldview commitment. I'm a Christian first because I believe it's true objectively. Subjectively, I've made a passionate faith commitment based on an ideal that I feel speaks uniquely to the human condition. But I would not be a Christian without a rational springboard (metaphysical arguments for God, historical basis for Christianity, etc.).

But enough about my metaphysics, let's discuss yours! We agree that certain actions are objectively wrong independent of a culture's tradition. We also agree you don't need to believe in God to have a moral sense or to act morally. Where I get lost with naturalism is on objective morality. As I stated earlier, in my view, God is Being and Goodness Itself. My conclusion that God exists is no different than my moral realism—they are the reasoned end of my metaphysical realism. You mentioned that "the great advantage of naturalism is that it asks us to believe only in things that can be measured, observed, and objectively experienced" and doesn't require one "to infer anything about physical reality from subjective, internal mental states."

As a naturalist and skeptic, can you dissect your secular humanism for me? How do you feel morality is objective? What is a unit of objective morality? Can you prove it for me empirically, please? Does naturalism coherently require secular humanism? Like all these bickering theologians, will naturalists continue to bicker on moral realism?

---

5. Kierkegaard, *Papers and Journals*, 32–33.

META

It was a great mistake to say that God made man in his image. Man, in all ages, made his God in his own image; and we find that just in accordance with his civilization, his knowledge, his experience, his taste, his refinement, his sense of right, of justice, or freedom, and humanity—so has he made his God. But whether coarse or refined; cruel and vindictive, or kind and generous; an implacable tyrant, or a gentle and loving father; it still was the emanation of his own mind—the picture of himself.[6]

—ERNESTINE L. ROSE, "A DEFENSE OF ATHEISM"

Andrew,

Thanks again for inviting me to take part in our radio debate last month. It was fun, even if I felt at times that I was arguing with the host more than with you! But that's fine with me: I welcome the chance to go into the lion's den, so to speak. What would be the point of defending atheism before an audience of people who mostly agree with me?

On the subject of how people acquire religious belief, I think this is mainly a question of what precedes what. I don't know what your personal story is, and if you believe that Christianity speaks uniquely to the human condition in a way that other religions don't, I'd like to hear why. But when I see someone first acquiring religious belief in childhood, or through a powerfully emotional conversion experience, and later using sophisticated apologetics to defend it, it sets my skeptical senses tingling. Human beings are very good at finding clever rationalizations for things we want to believe for other reasons, and the most obvious proof of this is that millions of people make the same arguments in support of completely different and incompatible faiths!

Since you brought up personal experience of God, let me cite an example that references what I mean. The essayist Andrew Sullivan, when he speaks of his own Catholic belief and how he came by it, describes it as "a revelation of God's love and forgiveness, the improbable notion that the force behind all of this actually loved us, and even loved me."[7] That sounds a lot like what you mentioned, except for one phrase that Sullivan chooses

---

6. Rose, "A Defense of Atheism," 73.
7. Sullivan, "Is Religion Built Upon Lies?" Samharris.org.

to describe his experience that I find quite revealing: he says it was a "voice with no words."

From what I've read of these religious experiences, that's typical of the genre. While rich in emotional color and texture, they're usually light on actual content. Instead, the believer experiences a variety of sensations: an oceanic feeling of transcendent bliss, a vivid sense of heightened significance and interconnection, a perception of being swept away from oneself or unified with the infinite. Yet there's hardly ever an audible voice or a clear message. (If God wants to communicate with us, why not do it in a physical body that could tangibly interact with the world?)

These encounters never cause a person to convert to a completely different religion which they were unfamiliar with prior to the experience. Instead, the religious experience is invariably interpreted as confirmation of a belief set which the person either already belonged to or was seriously considering converting to. These experiences are shaped and interpreted in light of upbringing and culture. Whenever and wherever they occur, they're always believed to be manifestations of the locally popular deity, whichever one that is.

I have no doubt that experiences like this are real, and that they often have a profound and lasting effect on the lives of people who have them. But that sense of rapture, like many other things, isn't confined to one religion and isn't even a solely religious experience: it's a human phenomenon found in every culture. If it were more widely known that believers of all sects have equally persuasive experiences of this kind—and if it were more widely known that atheists have them as well (yes, atheists also have moments of transcendent joy!)—then we might develop a more nuanced view of their causes.

But perhaps we'll revisit this later on. You asked about my views on morality, and I'm happy to oblige. As I mentioned earlier, I believe that the basis for morality is human happiness. It can't be otherwise, because if you start with any other virtue—justice, say, or filial duty, or patriotism, or individual liberty, or religious piety—you can ask why we should value that quality, why we should care about it at all. And whatever answer you give, you can ask the same question again. If you chase this regression all the way down, you'll ultimately end up at happiness: the only quality that's intrinsically valuable, the only thing we desire for its own sake and not because it gives rise to some other instrumental good.

Here's what I see as the most important step: the realization that happiness is an empirical phenomenon. Although individuals have unique likes and dislikes, there are basic, fixed facts about the human nature which we all have in common. This means that there are objective truths about what does and doesn't promote human well-being. These moral truths exist not by decree of a supernatural being, but simply by virtue of the kind of beings *we* are and the ways in which we relate to each other.

This means that not all opinions about morality are created equal; not all ideas about what promotes happiness are correct. Some are better than others, reflect reality more closely than others. And the only way to reliably identify those that are better and those that are worse is through rational debate and testing based on empirical evidence. That's the sense in which I'd say that morality is objective.

As I see it, the purpose of society is to ensure that everyone's basic needs are met, and then, as far as is practical, to get out of the way and make it possible for each person to pursue their own vision of the good life. In his book *The Moral Landscape*, Sam Harris invites us to imagine a landscape where every point stands for a particular way of organizing society, and the elevation of that point represents the happiness that that society produces. On this landscape there are foothills, ridges and mountain peaks, representing blissful utopias, and there are sinkholes, valleys and deep depressions, representing dystopias of various kinds—dictatorships, theocracies, oligarchies—where the well-being of the many is trampled for the sake of the few. Our task is to figure out how to move uphill: to find the innovations, whether they be technological, political or philosophical, that improve life for all of us.

Obviously, this is a very complex task, and I don't claim to have all the answers. I'd describe this proposal as a framework for approaching the issue, not a set of immutable commandments. But I think there are some fundamental moral truths that it would be sheer folly to deny. For example, because conscious existence is obviously a prerequisite for happiness, I agree that human life should be preserved whenever possible. To destroy another person, except in the direst cases of self-defense or to relieve otherwise unbearable suffering, is a terrible crime because it robs them of all the happiness they might otherwise have had.

I'd like to hear more about where we part company, but in general, I find that my views differ from religious believers in one of two ways. With some, I have a philosophical disagreement: the theists who believe that

Faith, Reason, and Morality, Part II

human happiness is *not* important, only God's happiness is, and therefore he's entitled to treat us however he sees fit. I think Calvinists could fairly be described as believing this, for example. (I remember once reading a tract that said that people in heaven and people in hell glorify God equally, just in different ways: the saved by making it possible for him to show his love, the damned by making it possible for him to show his wrath. That always gives me a shudder.)

Then there are the theists who believe that human happiness is paramount, but that there's an afterlife which is infinitely more significant than this one, and so our primary moral responsibility is to follow whatever rules have to be followed to secure access to the better class of afterlife. I think this view is less pernicious than the other, but I still have a fundamental disagreement with it: namely, that it denigrates the known at the expense of the unknown. It's often used to ask us to sacrifice our well-being in *this* life—the only one that we know for sure we have—for the sake of an ethereal, invisible other world, one that can't be explored or even shown to exist. Afterlife-based morality can produce good results for human beings, but when it does, it's only by coincidence. I'm curious to hear if you'd describe yourself as belonging to either of these camps, or if you'd advocate something different entirely.

ROUND 4

Metamorality and Applied Ethics, Part I

I do think that all men, including myself, are religious. We do all believe in something more—and it is difficult to find the right words—than ourselves. While I do not want to set up a new kind of faith, what we really believe in is what we call a Third World, something which is beyond us and with which we do interact, in the literal sense of interaction, and through which we can transcend ourselves.[1]

—KARL POPPER

Adam,

    It's always a pleasure doing live exchanges with you—here's to many, many more!

    On arriving at justified beliefs, we're both unimpressed by tribal ad hoc rationalizations and agree that "human beings are very good at finding clever rationalizations for things we want to believe for other reasons." Like you, such reasoning "sets my skeptical senses tingling." If theism hinged upon lit-up-cross sightings, I'd share your atheism. To be fair, moral objectivity hinging upon materialism sets my and many atheists' skeptical hairs tingling! On any belief system, the question for the truth seeker will always remain: on what rational foundation does such a belief rest? I agree that religious experience presents "an oceanic feeling of transcendent bliss, a

1. Popper, "Karl Popper on God," 49.

vivid sense of heightened significance and interconnection, a perception of being swept away from oneself or unified with the infinite." Upon a strong rational foundation for God, this is even more suggestive for those theistically inclined. I agree that all people, religious or irreligious, have these experiences and would love to explore this topic further with you. To your point on why God just doesn't communicate directly with the world in a physical body, this is ultimately addressed with Christianity, which is certainly on our list of topics to discuss.

To continue along with morality, I'll shape my reply by starting on points we agree. We're both moral realists and feel morality is objective. We agree that any sound moral philosophy requires considerable empirical and consequential (good of the whole) consideration. Unchecked dogmatic ideals, religious and irreligious, have led to some nasty endpoints. That said, I think we'd approach many moral dilemmas in the same way. As I've said at our debates, with the secular humanism you espouse, we agree on much with the *marketing* (practical ethics), just not the *accounting* (metaethics). To your question—do I feel human happiness and well-being is important? Of course: you're talking to an Aristotelian virtue theorist! And yes, of course whatever one defines as "happiness" or "well-being" (for example, how many people live without disease until ninety years of age) can be validated empirically.

But this is where we begin to part ways. Make no mistake—"morality is ultimately about well-being" is *a philosophical view*—one I know well! It's based on Aristotle's virtue theory, which you seem to endorse for its practicality ("for its own sake" and "by virtue of the kinds of beings *we* are and the ways in which we relate to each other"), though your materialism requires you to reject its hylomorphism and teleology (nature is irreducibly material and immaterial) which give virtue its metaphysical foundation for objectivity. To me, God is Goodness and Being Itself, so "well-being" without God (the ground of all being and goodness) becomes a subjective term. Consider the terms for a moment: happiness and well-being. We can empirically evaluate, validate, and verify specific hypotheses—this is the entirety of the scientific method. But the question remains: what is well-being and happiness? The metaphysical first principle is philosophical, not scientific. How do you maintain Aristotle's virtue theory, while at the same time rejecting his metaphysics? In other words, how is "Adam's view of morality" objective?

This is where secular humanism seems to me a case of metaphysical special-pleading, a halfway house between skepticism and deism. As you know, many naturalists are not secular humanists and feel that rejection of objective moral values, in the words of moral philosopher Richard Garner, "will be facilitated, if not forced, by the ease of which arguments used to undermine theism can be recycled to criticize the analogous beliefs of secular moralists."[2] Actually, it's been atheist, agnostic, and skeptic thinkers who I feel have made the most cogent arguments against ethical naturalism—specifically Hume's "is/ought problem," Moore's "open question" and "naturalistic fallacy," and Mackie's "queer facts." To briefly touch upon some of these—how could we attain knowledge of objective "goodness" from empirical investigation of natural properties? Moore's "naturalistic fallacy" labels it fallacious to equate a natural property (pleasure, happiness, etc.) with a moral property (goodness)—the "open question" objection is that this natural property is always *open to question*—"I know this makes me happy, but is it good?" Mackie's "queerness" objection holds it quite peculiar that there would be an objective moral ontology in natural properties—ones that motivate no less. Hume is even more direct—you cannot derive "ought" (subjective) from "is" (objective).[3]

Back to happiness and the limits of consequentialism. Allow me to propose what I've labelled "The Arctic Thought Experiment." It has been observed that Inuit tribes will kill their babies and elderly. As the situation is extreme and resources are limited, actions are taken to promote what could be labelled several things including "good of the whole," "well-being," and "happiness"—so let's explore that. Assume that the "contributing population," say it's 90 percent of the tribe, preys upon the remaining "weak" (babies and elderly). So babies are killed, fed to the sled dogs, and elderly are escorted to the cold to freeze to death. Imagine you wake up one day to discover that you're leader of the tribe. You could put a stop to this practice, but the net result would be only 40 percent survival of the tribe as the contributing population would be weighed down by the burden of the "weak" and suffer serious casualties in the process. *First question: what would you do?* Now, let's assume the tribe splits into two, Tribe A (100 people) and Tribe B (100 people). Tribe A discontinues the current practice and has forty survivors, while Tribe B continues the current practice and has sixty survivors. *Second question: which tribe is more moral?*

2. Garner, "Morality," *Philosophy Now*.
3. Campbell, "Moral Epistemology," *The Stanford Encyclopedia of Philosophy*.

Also, while we're on the topic of morality, do you feel we have a moral sense that is innate to each of us? Until our next cup of French Press coffee...

Such facts are the foundation of (the rest of) objective morality and rest on no foundation themselves. To ask of such facts, 'where do they come from?' or 'on what foundation do they rest?' is misguided in much the way that, according to many theists, it is misguided to ask of God, 'where does He come from?' or 'on what foundation does He rest?' The answer is the same in both cases: They come from nowhere, and nothing external to themselves grounds their existence; rather, they are fundamental features of the universe that ground other truths.[4]

ERIK WIELENBERG

Andrew,

 Just as we agree that morality is a real phenomenon with both rational and empirical components, I think there are moral skeptics among theists as well as among atheists. The theistic moral skeptics would be the people who believe that goodness consists solely of doing God's will, as interpreted by them at any given moment, even if it starkly contradicts what they previously believed. I'm sure you can come up with your own examples.

 You asked for a comprehensive definition of happiness, and I'll be the first to admit that I can't give you one. That's not surprising, because happiness is a quale: one of the irreducible, first-person mental states that define our state of conscious existence. Like other qualia, happiness has an ineffable quality. I can't define "redness" without reference to other concepts, but we're acquainted with it by direct experience and know it when we see it. I don't think this is special pleading so much as the inevitable circularity that lies at the bedrock of all conceptual systems. As I said, I ground my moral system by chasing down the regression of things we desire, until we arrive at the most basic desire, the one that isn't defined in terms of anything else.

 However, while we can't empirically define happiness, we *can* define and observe its correlates: good health and nutrition, stable employment, lack of poverty, meaningful social relationships, and all the other causes that feed into the multidimensional emotional state we know as happiness (or well-being, or satisfaction, or fulfillment, or any of the many other synonyms that differ in shadings of connotation).

---

4. Wielenberg, "In Defense of Non-Natural," 23–41.

Metamorality and Applied Ethics, Part I

When it comes to atheistic moral skeptics, I'm aware that I can't convince someone who disagrees with me on first principles. The only answer I can give them is the same answer anyone can give to any kind of philosophical skeptic: namely, a practical answer ("I refute it thus!"). Whatever we might say about the unknowability of reality, no one in their right mind would jump off a cliff because they believe the law of gravity is just someone's opinion. Similarly, whatever anyone says about morality being subjective, no one really wants to live in the anarchic world that would result if everyone acted as if this were true. No one wants strangers to decide whether to kiss you or kill you based on their whims; we want and expect everyone we encounter to act based on rules of conduct we all know and respect.

Then again, this is probably overstating the case. I think most self-proclaimed moral skeptics are perfectly good and decent people, and most of them make moral decisions the same way as I do. Our disagreement, I've found, is mainly a disagreement over language, not ontology—much like the question, "Are numbers real?" Depending on your definition of "real," two people may disagree fiercely about this, yet they can both calculate and arrive at the right answer.

In our discussion of utilitarianism, you proposed a thought experiment about an Inuit tribe living in harsh conditions that's facing starvation, and whose leader has to decide whether some people, like the elderly who can no longer help with the hunt, should be sent out into the wilderness to freeze so that there's more food for everyone else.

Daniel Dennett calls these kinds of thought experiments "intuition pumps,"[5] and when you encounter one of them, he suggests "twiddling the knobs"—changing some of the parameters to see if it's some underappreciated feature of the scenario itself that's doing the work. So, let's try that!

Let's say you're a doctor in a hospital emergency room, and two people with severe injuries are brought in at the same time. You have enough units of blood to save one of them, but *only* one of them. What do you do? Would you do nothing, rather than be forced to choose who lives and who dies? Or would you ineffectively divide the available blood supply among both patients, knowing that it wouldn't be enough to save either from death by blood loss? I suggest that either of those options are less moral than saving one person. If you find it unbearable to make that choice, you could flip a

---

5. Dennett, *Intuition Pumps and Other Tools for Thinking*.

coin or do something random. But when you can't save everyone, at least save *someone*, for goodness' sake!

If the Inuit scenario seems unthinkable, I'd suggest that it's because you and I have never had to make choices like that. I know my life has been privileged: I was born to a middle-class family in a wealthy, industrialized nation, and I've never gone hungry, much less had to seriously contemplate the prospect of starvation. Assuming your background is similar to mine, it's natural that we'd recoil in horror at having to make such a stark decision, in conditions of deprivation so unlike what either of us is used to.

To be clear, I don't think this scenario applies to *our* society, which has ample ability to care for the elderly and the disabled. But across most of history, the vast majority of people wouldn't find this scenario unrealistic at all. Poverty and deprivation have always forced people to make terrible sacrifices. I once read a story about a very poor family in Cambodia who had to choose which of their children would sleep under their family's only anti-malaria net each night.[6]

Morality doesn't dictate that there's always a *good* option. Sometimes, there's only a least-bad option. But I'd argue that part of what it means to be moral is that we do what good we can, save as many people as we can, rather than throw up our hands and surrender to fatalism if a catastrophe can't be entirely averted. To tie this back to the overarching theme of our debate, another part of what it means to be moral is working together and pooling our efforts for the common good, so that we don't *have* to face choices like this as often.

I think morality is "innate" in the sense that human beings are born with both a capacity for benevolent cooperation as well as a capacity for prejudice and violence. In that sense, good and evil are both equally innate in us. Our upbringing and circumstances have a lot to do with which one predominates. And again, this is why it's important to design good governmental systems to bring the good to the fore more often! Individual moral virtue is obviously something to be encouraged, but it's also unrealistic to expect everyone to display it all the time, regardless of their circumstances. It's much better to create an environment where goodness can more easily flourish.

If you'd like to talk more about morality, I'm up for that. Otherwise, there's something you hinted at that I'd like to follow up on. You said that one's choice of religion is an irrational leap of faith, yet you also maintain

6. Kristof, "Wretched."

that Christianity is in some way a distinctive religious worldview. I'm curious to hear how you reconcile these statements.

ROUND 5

Metamorality and Applied Ethics, Part II

The important thing is not to stop questioning. Curiosity has its own reason for existing. One cannot help but be in awe when he contemplates the mysteries of eternity, of life, of the marvelous structure of reality. It is enough if one tries merely to comprehend a little of this mystery every day. Never lose a holy curiosity.

—ALBERT EINSTEIN

Adam,

I'm thrilled that we've expanded our debate series to the Big Apple! For this one, you will certainly have home court advantage, but I have the momentum if there's a ping pong rematch, though I must admit I barely escaped with a 3-2 victory last time and you gave me all I could handle!

To gather up some last thoughts on morality, we agree on objective moral truth, the value of empiricism, and that any sound moral theory requires a significant consequential endpoint (though we disagree on the limits). We're also aligned with morality having an innate component where certain virtues are self-evident, yet tradition, culture, and circumstances having a strong influence on their expression (e.g., Nazi soldiers shared humanity's common moral hardwiring; they just didn't extend it to Jews).

Unsurprisingly, a major area of disagreement for us is on moral ontology. As I mentioned earlier, the landmark criticisms (Hume's is/ought problem, Moore's naturalistic fallacy and open question argument, and Mackie's queer facts) clearly reveal the bankruptcy of moral ontology and objectivity from the naturalistic worldview. The problem with ontology, as stated by philosopher Michael Smith, is that "it is distinctive of moral practice that we are concerned to get the answers to moral questions right. But this concern presupposes that there are correct answers to moral questions to be had."[1] If naturalism is true, how can there be an objective good? What is it? In Peter Singer's words,

> There have been many attempts, over the centuries, to find proofs of first principles in ethics, but most philosophers consider that they have failed. Even a radical theory like utilitarianism must rest on a fundamental intuition about what is good. So we appear to be left with our intuitions, and nothing more. If we reject them all, we must become ethical skeptics or nihilists.[2]

On your intuition on what is good, your definition of happiness is ultimately an "irreducible, first-person mental state." Earlier you stated that "the great advantage of naturalism is that it asks us to believe only in things that can be measured, observed, and objectively experienced" and that it doesn't require anyone "to infer anything about physical reality from subjective, internal mental states." If I were a naturalist, why exactly is "Adam's views on morality" objective? Your definition goes beyond what naturalism requires.

Of consequence, I would take issue with your point on moral skepticism—that your view and those of moral skeptics is just a disagreement on language and not ontology. Certainly, many moral skeptics are decent people and reason in a *pragmatically* similar way to moral realists. But make no mistake, moral skepticism directly conflicts with ethical naturalism ontologically.

To your position, moral philosopher Sharon Street would argue just the opposite, that the consequence of naturalism is normative bankruptcy, and that we ultimately construct our own normative judgements, measured by our own standards. "Happiness," if we peeled back the onion, would simply be a list of Adam's "evaluative attitudes."[3]

Relativists may agree with you that "morality exists," but imply its truths are, in the words of moral philosopher Jesse Prinz, "culturally

---

1. Smith, "Realism," 399.
2. Singer, "Ethics and Intuitions," 349.
3. Street, "Constructivism about Reasons," 207–45.

conditioned" (there are many truths, not an objective one). To the Arctic Thought Experiment, one may say Tribe A is moral, while someone else claims Tribe B is moral, but there can be no objectivity given the "normative emptiness of evolution."[4]

Moral error theorists think morality is a category error to begin with. There is no morality. They would grant that Tribe A may have *more survival* than Tribe B, but the last thing they would do would call either tribe *moral/immoral*. In this camp, Richard Joyce, a "moral fictionalist," labels moral truth and objectivity as fictions, illusory side-effects of our evolutionary past (nature) and cultural conditioning (nurture)—we have the perfect illusion. You and I say there are objective right and wrong answers; error theorists think we simply need to grow up. In Joyce's words:

> This enterprise of self-exoneration can seem immature, as deriving from an anxious need for reassurance. . . . By the time we take our first tottering steps, each of us is already immersed in a social world rich in concepts like *right* and *wrong*. . . . Our childhood is one grand advertising campaign designed to get us to internalize these concepts and take them seriously—a campaign, moreover, that in all likelihood we are biologically designed to find compelling, because thinking in this fashion helped our ancestors produce more babies than their competitors. And so we do. Nowhere, however, does this account of how we come to make moral judgments presuppose that any beliefs in question are actually true (even approximately so). Now, as adult philosophers—being in a position to stand back and see the process for what it is—do we really need to concoct cunning theories designed to earn this missing truth for our moral beliefs?"[5]

These views are in serious conflict with any naturalist who maintains morality is objective. Certainly, we could all sit down and agree *pragmatically* on some core principles for the "functional city" (social contracts, laws, etc.). But what you and I might call "the just and moral city"—the relativist would say ask the locals and an error theorist like Joyce would smile and nod at "just and moral," but really hold they are fictitious terms (aiming at nothing ontologically).

Along these lines, moral psychologists like Josh Greene and Jonathan Haidt share a similar skepticism on your intuitions on happiness. Psychological and neuroscientific evidence shows that our emotions drive our

---

4. Prinz, "Morality is a Culturally Conditioned Response."
5. Joyce "Moral Fictionalism," *Philosophy Now*.

judgements and actions. We rationalize only after emotional judgements/actions are made (Haidt) or at best we *try* (quite partially) to rationally balance our first, automatic, emotional instincts (Greene).[6] Both researchers are atheists and moral skeptics. The last thing they see, given their naturalism and research on moral cognition, is moral ontology and objectivity.

But wait, that's where science comes in! Back to another key area of agreement—the right answer is frequently not obvious, nor should it be grappled with only from the armchair. Science attempts to provide an objective *method* of testing a hypothesis. But what is our measure, our virtue, our intuition about what's good? We're highly fallible, biased, and limited, so we agree there needs to be a "check and balance." But with your views on happiness, what are we measuring? Is it just pleasure measured by the net amount of serotonin of each society? Is it just hedonism? Is it just maximizing survival at all costs?

That is where The Arctic Thought Experiment comes in. We agree that neither of us have been in such a crisis, so we cannot fully comprehend the gravity of such a reality. But let's try. If I did wake up to find myself in that situation, I would strive to do what is "just." At the end of my thought experiment, I offered that the tribe (200 people) splits into Tribe A (100 people) and Tribe B (100 people). Tribe A discontinues the current practice and has forty survivors, while Tribe B continues the current practice and has sixty survivors. In surviving off the backs (quite literally) of the vulnerable, my argument is that we can't call Tribe B "more moral," just the opposite.

I like your thought experiment! So, there I am, the emergency room doctor, two people bleeding to death and I only have enough blood to save one. We agree that it would be immoral not to save one individual. We'd have to modify your thought experiment, though, to stay consistent with mine. Let's assume Person A and Person B are middle-aged identical twins, both doctors themselves with rare blood types, and there is no available blood in storage. You do the best you can and start injecting "investigational plasma" to allow for very short-term survival. The nurse is calling all the blood banks and the situation looks bleak. Now, you learn there are two patients in the hospital with the same blood type, one infant and one elderly patient, the infant abandoned by the birth mother and the elderly patient with no surviving kin. The amount of blood available from the infant and elderly patient is just enough should we elect to drain all their blood

---

6. Singer, "Ethics and Intuitions," 331–52.

(obviously killing them) and transfusing that blood to save the emergency room doctor's patients. Let's assume this is a country where such actions are legal and the decision is ultimately yours—the "contributing members of society" or the infants and elderly patients?

My point with both thought experiments is to illustrate the limits of consequentialism. Moral armchair reasoning can be quite frightening, consequentialism included. Again, there needs to be a "check and balance" between reason and empiricism. Nevertheless, at the end of the day, all moral philosophies are measured by the virtue of their own first principle. And so, we're back to metaphysics!

In my view, God is Being and Goodness Itself, so acting "well" is ultimately about reaching one's potential as a rational animal. Basic well-being (basic physical needs, not murdering others, etc.) will hardly be a point of contention for most of us. But on a deeper level, what is good and the highest good is ultimately built upon one's metaphysics. From the vantage point of naturalism, I agree with Dawkins that ours would simply be a "universe of electrons and selfish genes, blind physical forces and genetic replication.... No purpose, no evil and no good. Nothing but blind pitiless indifference.... DNA neither knows nor cares. DNA just is, and we dance to its music."[7] Certainly, we can *subjectivize* meaning, laws, and moral first principles, but they are far from objective.

Beyond a generic theism and natural law, this is where Christianity comes in for me. To me, the Golden Rule, "what you do to the least of these, you do to Me" (Matt 25:40), and living/dying for others as presented in the example of Christ define the "highest good." I will not pretend to know the "highest good" in every case, but I attempt to live virtuously in trying to follow this example. So yes, I do feel that Christianity is a distinct worldview. And no, one's choice of religion is not just an "irrational leap of faith" unless of course it's a belief with no rational foundation. True, the faith dimension—the experience of God, subjective faith commitment, existential embrace of the ideal—surpasses reason. But remember, Christianity involves both reason and faith, which I feel both have distinct elements. Theologically, I feel it's a unique revelation about the nature of God and humanity. Rationally, I feel it has a unique springboard that combines the rationality of theism and God's existence in general with a historical foundation. As the exchange continues, we can certainly discuss why I'm touched theologically by the Christian narrative. I've given you plenty on the classical

---

7. Dawkins, *River Out of Eden*, 133.

metaphysical arguments for God's existence. For now, I'll expand upon the historicity of Christianity in my reply.

META

Long-haired preachers come out every night
Try to tell you what's wrong and what's right
But when asked how 'bout something to eat
They will answer in voices so sweet
You will eat, by and by
In that glorious land above the sky
Work and pray, live on hay
You'll get pie in the sky when you die

—JOE HILL, "THE PREACHER AND THE SLAVE"

Andrew,

Thanks again for making the trip out to Long Island. I thought the turnout for our second live debate was excellent! I was pleasantly surprised by how many people told us we should do this again, so maybe that's something to consider for the future.

To address your permutation of the emergency-room doctor thought experiment (which I note is similar to the philosophers' infamous "trolley problem"), I'd contend that it's wrong to deliberately kill someone who would otherwise have lived to save the life of someone in danger of dying. But when a group of people all share the same danger of dying, it's not wrong to sacrifice some so that others may live. This is just the principle of "double effect" that philosophers have propounded for a long time, which says that there's a difference between unwanted but unavoidable harm versus planned and intended harm.

I'd agree that any moral philosophy, if taken to extremes, can produce horrific results. That's true of both religious and secular philosophies. But what I'd say is that morality has to have a reality check. However beautiful its reasoning or elegant its axioms, every moral philosophy has to be evaluated based on whether it benefits or harms real people. Any moral system that is derived wholly from inflexible first principles, without looking at the world to see how it plays out, can lead to bad results, whether it's consequentialist, deontological, or something else entirely.

I agree as well that Jonathan Haidt and other social scientists have shown how emotion can overpower reason in human cognition. We human beings are fallible creatures, no doubt about it! That's *why* it's so important to have a morality that's empirically based; that, like the scientific method, works against our biases rather than giving them free rein, and relies on evidence and rational persuasion as much as possible. However, that doesn't mean that we have to nail down every possible ambiguity before we can begin reasoning morally, or that we have to define "happiness" in rigorously objective, mathematically precise terms. In the same way, "health" doesn't have a mathematically precise, one-size-fits-all definition, and yet that doesn't impede doctors from working to make sick people well. In both cases, it's usually perfectly obvious what needs to be done.

Just to be clear, I'm not saying that morality is always easy! Many moral disputes are among the most complex and intractable problems that humanity faces. What I *am* saying is that the framework I've proposed offers a guide, a road map if you will, for getting to the bottom of them. When two people disagree about morality, if they share the principle that happiness is the ultimate aim, they can compare their evidences, debate the best angle to approach the problem, point out any interests or concerns the other side's analysis fails to account for, and eventually come to a conclusion.

By contrast, an ethical system based on the supernatural is intrinsically unmoored from reality. When people rely on the unverifiable word of a deity as the basis for their morality, it becomes far too easy to pass off gut feelings and irrational emotional reactions as divine commandments. That's something we saw with, for example, the debate over same-sex marriage, where millions of people who have an instinctive feeling of revulsion towards homosexuality treat it as a definitive communication from God. In a religious moral system, that's all you need. Whoever can more confidently assert their belief in what God wants usually carries the day. In a secular moral system, you can't stop there; you'd have to justify that feeling on the basis of objective reasons before you could build law and policy around it.

And when two people disagree about what God's will is, there's no way to settle the question. Even sharing common beliefs about God doesn't help, as history shows plainly that people who use the same holy book and believe in the same deity can have diametrically opposed opinions about what he expects from human beings. People who theoretically belong to the same religion have been on opposite sides of the question when it comes to slavery, women's suffrage, civil rights, democracy, LGBT rights, immigration, environmental conservation, contraception and abortion, pacifism versus militarism, and virtually every other great moral controversy of the past and present. I'd wager this is something you have personal experience with, probably more than I do. Personally, I could go on about the roots of morality forever. But since I think we've pretty well delineated our areas of agreement and disagreement, I'd like to suggest we move on to the distinctiveness of Christianity next.

I'll lay my cards on the table: I think Christianity, like all faiths, is a product of its time and place. It's a recognizable amalgam of two religious traditions, namely Hellenistic-influenced Judaism and the pagan mystery cults that taught salvation through ritual sacrifice, and it arose at the time and place that those streams of thought were mingling, at a cosmopolitan crossroads of the Roman Empire.

As you know from our live debates, I believe that Jesus of Nazareth was a mythological figure, not a historical human being. The New Testament Gospels are our most detailed source of biographical information about him, but they're also anonymous, contradict each other on many important points, and contain material clearly drawn from legendary-hero allegories or Old Testament midrash. Mentions of Jesus in the writings of Jewish and Roman historians are late, scanty on detail, and are generally based on what Christians believed in any case.

The usual secular explanation is that Jesus was a historical person who was later elevated to divinity, but I think the process happened in reverse. I'd argue that there's evidence that Jesus Christ *started out* as a spiritual savior figure, similar to the redeemer gods of the mystery religions, who later acquired the characteristics of a mortal man and was retroactively inserted into history.

If this strikes you as bizarre, we can see the same thing happening in new and emerging religions today. The cargo cult of John Frum on the Pacific island of Tana or the folk religion of Jesus Malverde the Narcosaint in Sinaloa, Mexico are two recent examples. Both arose within the last few decades, and both believe in a founder figure who combines human qualities with mythological or supernatural attributes, and whose real historical existence is deemed cloudy or dubious by outside historians who've investigated the matter.

As far as the actual teachings attributed to Jesus, I find things to like and things to dislike. I'm all for the teachings about loving one another, showing compassion, and helping the needy. These are good ideas common to many cultures. But I'm disturbed by Jesus' equally numerous teachings about the imminence of the apocalypse, which have always been used to justify turning away from this world and delaying efforts to establish earthly justice.

The great American freethinker Robert Ingersoll put it best when said that Jesus' most serious moral flaw was that he believed in hell. For all the cruelties of the Old Testament, it never envisioned further punishment after death. It was Christianity that introduced this idea into the Western religious tradition, the idea that those who don't worship God in accordance with his commands will be condemned to an afterlife of infinite suffering. I think this is the most evil teaching there is, and it's always been used to dehumanize and demonize outsiders and treat them as worthy only of destruction.

This is a very quick summary of my position, but it's enough to turn it over to you for the reply. Can you expand on why you find Christianity to be historically plausible or theologically distinctive?

ROUND 6

Philosophical Theism and Christianity, Part I

Neuroscience itself appears to be unable to provide information regarding the ultimate level of reality, whether that level is called God, nirvana, or AUB (Absolute Unitary Being).... Reality happens in our brain, and while our imaging studies do not prove the existence of a higher spiritual plane, they do strongly indicate that to the brain, these states are as real as any other.... Time and time again, people who experience intense mystical states insist that these states feel more real than everyday reality. Neurology can neither prove nor disprove this point, but informed speculation tells us that it's possible that AUB may be as real, if not more fundamentally real, than what we perceive as 'ordinary' reality.... It may even be the case that the state of AUB is a primary reality, one from which all objective and subjective perspectives of the world are derived. Whether or not AUB is ontologically real, it provides us with a common source of all spiritual urges and a universal goal that has been interpreted in a myriad of ways by all the great religions of the past and present.[1]

—ANDREW NEWBERG, *WHY GOD WON'T GO AWAY*

Adam,

We could certainly go on forever on the subject of morality. We agree that people of the same religious position have been on opposite sides of

---

1. Newberg, *Why God Won't Go Away*, 178.

slavery, equality, democracy, environmental conservation, and "every other great moral controversy of the past." The same is true for the irreligious, so I'm enthused that we agree that moral questions are objectively truth-apt and that moral reasoning needs to be balanced by empirical validation. As we both commented, unchecked moral philosophies have led to some horrific endpoints.

I've relayed that my worldview is not immune to doubt (far from it), yet I find it unique. Why, you ask? It combines three key elements that I cannot deny: generic theism, historical strength, and theological appeal.

Generic Theism (Rationality of Theism and Experience of God)

As I've mentioned prior, it has to start with theism. We all have what Luigi Giussani eloquently labels "the religious sense."[2] For me, God is the sound end of philosophical reasoning as well as the actual source of spirituality and the first-person experience of transcendent wonder. Rationally, given existence, starting with why anything exists at all, then considering nature as a whole, and arriving at *our* existence—our conscious, rational, moral, transcendent, and seemingly spiritual selves—should we be inclined metaphysically to believe in Being and Goodness Itself, the ground of all being and goodness, the Prime Mover, Final Cause, and ultimate source of transcendence? Or, can we naturalize the seemingly metaphysical dimensions of our existence and humanity?

Neuroscientist Andrew Newberg argues that whether we like it or not, we have "metaphysical minds," that causality plays a "central role in human thought," and that causal reasoning is detectable in infants three to six months old. Aristotle postulated teleology in nature (material, efficient, formal, and final causes) and our metaphysical minds, with a flair for causal reasoning, are drawn to final causes, ends, and purposes (even if there are none).[3] The utility of causal reasoning has not only played a major role in our intellectual achievements, but our survival as a whole. We're far from infallible in this regard, but we have the neural mechanisms in place to seek causal truth for a number of aims. In Newberg's words:

> When causality is applied to the physical world, the result is science. When causality is applied to the human world, the result is

---

2. Giussani, *The Religious Sense*.
3. Newberg, *The Metaphysical Mind*, 82–92.

social science, psychology, and ethics. And when causality is applied to issues of ultimate concern such as existence, the universe, or god, the result is philosophy, theology, or religion. Thus, causal functions of the brain enable us to question why we are here, why something works the way it does, and what created the universe.[4]

Causal reasoning is an integral part of what Newberg labels "neurotheology" but perhaps even more powerful is the subjective first-person experience of God, those transcendent moments that you touched on in New York. At the level of the brain, we all have this transcendent religious sense.

Some amazing things are happening in the brain during these religious moments. It's metaphysically accounting for those phenomena where things get sticky. And here's the rub. One can certainly attempt to naturalize our metaphysical "inclinations" but as I mentioned with morality, I think the baby goes out with the bath water. Alex Rosenberg, for example, argues that the logical consequence of naturalism is to reject all these spooky ontologies—no God or Platonic realm, no objective morality, not even free will for that matter.[5] Moral ontology, like God, consciousness, and free will, is illusory. Our causal reasoning and metaphysical schemes are certainly suggestive, but they're simply side effects of our evolutionary past. Spirituality and the first-person experience of God are no different.

Are those transcendent moments that are occurring in the brain ultimately illusory, just Darwinian side effects that have selected for spirituality? Or, are they aiming finitely at something infinite? I say the latter. If I felt naturalism better accounted for the religious sense (philosophical reasoning and spiritual transcendence), I would certainly move in that direction. Moved rationally to a generic God of the Philosophers and transcendently to a very real experience of God, I am naturally open to consider a specific faith tradition. But it must be for good reason or else I would remain in an impersonal theism.

Historical Strength

Your theory certainly provokes conversation—it's certainly innovative, my friend! As you've admitted at our debates, you're in the vast minority of historical scholarship in holding to the fact that Jesus didn't exist. You're

---

4. Newberg, *Principles of Neurotheology*, 75–76.
5. Rosenberg, *The Atheist's Guide to Reality*, 7,14.

in luck though! I've considered it myself. Could a group of power-hungry social revolutionists just have concocted a new religious order, putting the new man-God (one the actually never existed) on their side?

A few things to consider. First, would be prominent New Testament scholar and agnostic Bart Ehrman's sentiments:

> I don't think there is any serious historian who doubts the existence of Jesus. . . . Why not just deny the Holocaust? . . . Why not deny Abraham Lincoln lived? . . . We have more evidence for Jesus than we have for almost anybody from His time period.[6]

The point here is that outside the Gospels, we have multiple independent attestations (Jewish and Roman—Tacitus, Josephus, Suetonius, and Pliny the Younger to name a few) to the life, ministry, following, and crucifixion of Jesus under Pilate. True, even for those that grant Jesus existed, did some "startling deeds," and was killed, one could wonder (as I have), was this just a power grab for the early followers to lead the charge with this new religion? But then I turn to the fact that we have multiple independent reports of the incredible persecution of the early followers who were tortured and murdered for their beliefs. I get that it was cool to wear Vans sneakers and listen to alternative music in the '90s (which I admit freely I experimented with) but it was not cool to worship a man-God in first-century Jewish-Roman culture. Contrary to your position, I cannot find any faith tradition that holds a candle to Christianity in terms of historical reliability. Not just the historical Jesus, but the historical footprint of the early church. For the early followers to give their lives to this cause—the only other explanation that I have seriously considered has been mass hallucination theory, but even that has serious problems.

Theological Appeal

We agree on the very moving and inspirational aspects of Christianity such as the Golden Rule, loving others, and charity. I am also very much moved by the idea of God entering into human history, dying for all of humanity, and validating the intrinsic worth of all people.

You mentioned hell is disturbing. To that, I agree and assure you that all believers have reflected deeply on this. You mentioned that you're repulsed by the idea of those "who don't worship God in accordance with his

---

6. Ehrman, Interview with Finley, The Infidel Guy Show.

commands will be condemned to an afterlife of infinite suffering" and that "it's been used to dehumanize and demonize outsiders and treat them as worthy only of destruction."

Just to be fair to the conversation, afterlife theology is a hotly debated item within Christianity and whether the Scriptures imply traditional hell (infinite separation from God), universalism (reconciliation with God for all), or annihilationist theory (soul death). Each of these is no doubt a wildly different theological interpretation.

To address the heart of your point, we agree that a rule-based salvation is repugnant and that many Christians have reduced their faith to judging others, so I think it's crucial to point out that heart of Christianity is Jesus as the exemplar of grace, humility, and inclusion. It is not rules, but grace, so there should not be boasting or judgement (Eph 2:8–9). When Jesus was pressed as to which laws were the most important, loving God and others was the reply (Matt 34–40). The law is now love; salvation is now grace. Thus, mine is the position that if Christianity is true, ours is a God more than worthy of loving, but I freely admit my unease with hell. I can only grant that if God exists, there is a metaphysical reality way beyond our epistemological pay grades of which the "religious sense" can only finitely grasp.

So my friend, I have to pose the metaphysical/spiritual questions back to you. Do you ever doubt your doubt and find yourself in a curious Prime Mover/spiritual mood? From why anything exists at all, to a seemingly teleological view of nature, to consciousness to free will to objective morality to transcendent "religious experience"—do you ever find yourself scratching your head at whether these phenomena are actually aiming at something beyond matter—not an elementary "god of the gaps," but on the entirety of existence and human experience, a "religious sense" highly suggestive of God's existence?

Convince me that Jesus didn't exist and I'll certainly reject Christianity. Convince me that on the totality of existence and our "metaphysical minds," that naturalism and secular humanism is stronger than theism or skepticism (baby out with the bathwater metaphysical skepticism of Rosenberg's type), and we'll stand together.

Philosophical Theism and Christianity, Part I

It is a natural human tendency to explain the development of progressive ideas, new technologies, better social and political systems, as the product of exceptional individuals, idealized forerunners, sometimes even as proceeding from divinities. The reality is typically otherwise. Society as a whole or a group within it produces the innovation or the swing in a new direction. . . . Eventually, these developments become attached in the popular or sectarian mind to a famous figure in their past, or embodied in an entirely fictitious personality.[7]

—EARL DOHERTY, *THE JESUS PUZZLE*

Andrew,

I think we should consider ourselves fortunate to live in an era when we've begun to pull back the curtain and get the first glimpses of what's really going on in that mysterious organ inside our heads. I've enjoyed reading about the work of scientists like Andrew Newburg who've helped to push back that frontier. I have no quibble with his factual findings, but I might offer a different interpretation of the metaphysics.

You suggested that, in some sense, we're all religious. As you might imagine, I'd consider that to be giving the game away at the beginning! I'd put it a different way: it's not that everyone is religious, but rather, that every human being has moments of transcendent wonder, mystery, and awe. I've experienced these peak moments myself: standing beneath a warm shower of rain in a tropical forest, or contemplating the misty band of the Milky Way on a dark clear night, or reading some elegantly perfect piece of writing or listening to some music so rapturously beautiful that it transports me temporarily outside myself.

What these moments have in common is that they give us a sense of connectedness to something larger and deeper, something that's both above us and all around us. Religion channels these feelings by providing an explanation that's based on the presumed will of supernatural beings. But these feelings aren't unique to religious people—they're common to all human beings—and the religious hypothesis isn't the only way to account for them.

---

7. Doherty, *The Jesus Puzzle*, 7.

META

I'd say that this is what we feel in those moments when we confront our own smallness in both space and time compared to the vast sweep of the cosmos, the fragility of the little circle of firelight we call our home, and the knowledge that in spite of it all, our minds are capable of grasping this totality, even to a limited degree. It's the pleasurable paradox of knowing that we're utterly insignificant compared to these things, and yet in a sense we stand above them by virtue of our understanding, that gives us the feeling of mind-blown humility and awe.

On that note, let's turn to the evidence against the historical existence of Jesus. I appreciate your tongue-in-cheek compliment on the "innovative" nature of my hypothesis, although I'd be the first to admit I didn't come up with this idea myself. It's a position that's long been entertained by freethinkers and other unorthodox scholars and historians. I'll grant that it goes against the grain of mainstream thought, but I think the fact that the historicity of Jesus is so rarely questioned is itself one of the things that makes it a promising ground for skeptical examination. You wrote:

> Your theory certainly provokes conversation—it's certainly innovative, my friend! As you've admitted at our debates, you're in the vast minority of historical scholarship in holding to the fact that Jesus didn't exist.

I agree that most biblical historians believe in the real historicity of Jesus. But I think this is what the skeptic Earl Doherty calls a "consensus of necessity." Many of these historians are Christians themselves, who have an obvious reason to reject a conclusion that would run contrary to their beliefs. Even for the ones who aren't, it would undermine their entire field of inquiry and call into question what they'd been doing with their careers this whole time.

You mentioned Bart Ehrman as one of them. I've enjoyed many of Bart Ehrman's books, but I think that on this point he's flat-out wrong. The idea that we have as much or more historical evidence for Jesus' existence as we do for anyone else from that time period just isn't true, and he knows it. For many Roman emperors and officials, for example, there are contemporary depictions on sculptures and coins; inscriptions that they personally commissioned; multiple, detailed biographies by disinterested historians; and events, like military conquests, that can't be explained unless *someone* carried them out. (By comparison, as skeptics have pointed out, there's nothing that would be accomplished by a resurrection that wouldn't also be accomplished by mere belief in a resurrection.) The most comparable evidence in Jesus' case are the Gospels: late, anonymous records, which contradict each other on numerous points.

You said:

> My point is that outside the Gospels, we have multiple independent attestations (Jewish and Roman—Tacitus, Josephus, Suetonius, Pliny the Younger to name a few) . . .

As one of the commenters on your website pointed out, you said "to name a few," giving the impression that there are more sources you could have cited. But in fact, those four brief mentions constitute the *entirety* of extra-biblical references to Jesus by ancient historians. So let's examine them.

Josephus: a Jewish historian working under Roman patronage, whose books contain two passages that mention Jesus. This is the longer one, the so-called Testimonium Flavianum:

> Now there was about this time, Jesus, a wise man, if it be lawful to call him a man, for he was a doer of wonderful work, a teacher of such men as receive the truth with pleasure. He drew over to him both many of the Jews, and many of the Gentiles. He was the Christ; and when Pilate, at the suggestion of the principal men amongst us, had condemned him to the cross, those that loved him at first did not forsake him, for he appeared to them alive again the third day, as the divine prophets had foretold these and ten thousand other wonderful things concerning him; and the tribe of Christians, so named after him, are not extinct at this day.[8]

The problem with this, as ought to be obvious, is that it's clearly written by a Christian. It praises Jesus as a miracle worker and the messiah, something that would have been inconceivable for either a Jewish historian or a client of the Roman rulers to say. Most historians consider this a devotional passage inserted into the manuscript by a later Christian copyist.

Josephus's other reference is to someone named James, whom he offhandedly mentions had a brother named Jesus:

> Festus was now dead, and Albinus was put upon the road; so he [Ananus, the Jewish high priest] assembled the Sanhedrin of judges, and brought before them the brother of Jesus, him called Christ, whose name was James, and some others. And when he

---

8. Josephus, *Antiquities*, Book 18, Chapter 3.

had formed an accusation against them as breakers of the law, he delivered them to be stoned . . .⁹

If we reject the Testimonium Flavianum as the obvious forgery it is, this is the only use of the term "Christ" in Josephus's writing, and it stands isolated, without explanation. It seems hard to believe that a careful historian would have casually dropped in such a consequential claim without elaboration. Josephus *does* write about someone else named Jesus in that same chapter: "Jesus, the son of Damneus" who succeeded Ananus as high priest. It seems very possible that a Christian copyist, who mistakenly thought the passage was about the Jesus he knew, made that connection himself by inserting the "him called Christ" phrase.

Suetonius: a Roman biographer and historian. He wrote a brief passage around 120 CE that doesn't actually mention Jesus at all, but says that the Jews of Rome had rioted at the instigation of someone named "Chrestus." Christian apologists have assumed, on the basis of no evidence I'm aware of, that this is a misspelled reference to Jesus Christ, even though "Chrestus" is a perfectly valid Latin name in its own right, and even though Suetonius says it was Jews who were rioting, not Christians (and yes, he knew the difference).

Pliny the Younger: a Roman official who wrote a letter to the emperor around 112 CE reporting that Christians were singing hymns to Christ, "as to a god." However, he says nothing about whether this was a historical human being or even whether the Christians believed he was.

Tacitus: another Roman historian who mentions around 115 CE that Christians were persecuted by Nero, and says that the sect was founded by a preacher called Christ who was crucified by Pilate:

> Consequently, to get rid of the report [that he was responsible for the great fire], Nero fastened the guilt and inflicted the most exquisite tortures on a class hated for their abominations, called Christians by the populace. Christus, from whom the name had its origin, suffered the extreme penalty during the reign of Tiberius at the hands of one of our procurators, Pontius Pilatus . . .¹⁰

This is the only extra-biblical historical reference to Jesus that depicts him unambiguously as a historical person and that clearly isn't an interpolation by Christian copyists. However, it was also written nearly a hundred

---

9. Josephus, *Antiquities*, Book 20, Chapter 9.
10. Tacitus, *Annals*, 15.44.

Philosophical Theism and Christianity, Part I

years after the events it purports to record. This is more than enough time for myth to become mingled with fact. It would be like someone writing about World War I in 2015, based solely on handed-down testimonials. The probable explanation is that Tacitus simply asked some Christians what they believed and wrote down what they told him. In short, this represents biblical material slowly migrating into the historical record.

When you examine this evidence in its totality, what's bound to strike you is how late-arising and scanty it really is. And it's not as if the idea of a spiritual savior figure being turned into a historical human being would be without precedent. In my previous letter, I mentioned two recent cases: John Frum, allegedly an American soldier who's believed to be the messiah by a cargo cult on the Pacific island of Tanna, and Jesus Malverde the Narcosaint, a Robin Hood-like bandit figure worshipped in certain parts of Mexico and believed to do miracles on behalf of drug smugglers and the poor. In both cases, it's uncertain whether there was any single historical person who stands at the origin of the legends, despite efforts by contemporary historians to investigate and find out what really happened.

And *these* cases happened less than a hundred years ago, in a world of universal literacy and mass media. Just think of how much easier it would have been for a legend to arise in the world of two millennia ago, where there were no cameras or newspapers, no birth certificates or Social Security numbers, where oral tradition and gossip were the only ways information could be passed around, and where the vast majority of people were uneducated and credulous. Imagine how easily rumor could seep into history, and spiritual beliefs could become clothed in flesh.

It's true, as historians like Tacitus record, that early Christians were tortured and executed for their beliefs. This often happened in the ancient world to all kinds of people. The Roman Empire wasn't known for its tolerance. But that doesn't say anything about what those beliefs actually were, or whether the people dying for them were in any position to know for certain whether they were true. We have many modern examples of people who've gone to their deaths for reasons that are bound to strike outsiders as utterly inadequate if not preposterous. Remember the Hale-Bopp comet cult mass suicide?

You mentioned the "historical footprint" of the early church, but what is that footprint, exactly? For instance, take the twelve apostles: those legendary figures, handpicked by Jesus, who supposedly stand at the dawn of Christianity. If you'd expect anyone to be well-documented, it's these fellows. Yet we know essentially nothing about where they lived, what they did, or how they died. There's not a single trustworthy historical source, just late-arising and often contradictory legends. All of them vanish into obscurity as soon as they pass out of the pages of the Gospels.

While I don't want to belabor the point, I want to emphasize that the mythicist theory isn't based solely on absences of evidence. It's also rooted in positive evidence: anomalies in the Christian record that the standard historicist picture doesn't account for very well.

Both many New Testament epistles and the writings of some first-century apologists seem to have been authored by people who are unfamiliar with the gospel story. Paul says that Christians don't know how to pray as they should (Rom 8:26), but hasn't he heard of the Lord's Prayer? He says that rulers hold no terrors to those who do good (Rom 13:3–4), but wasn't he supposed to be a follower of a man whose death serves as a potent counterexample?

Many early Christian writers describe their belief in the Son, or the Logos, God's divine creative force, but fail to mention that this cosmic entity ever walked the earth in human form. Often, they describe Jesus as a "spirit" or speak of him in ethereal terms. Here's one of the best examples, a passage written by a second-century Christian apologist named Minucius Felix:

> For in that you attribute to our religion the worship of a criminal and his cross, you wander far from the neighborhood of the truth, in thinking either that a criminal deserved, or that an earthly being was able, to be believed God.[11]

* * *

To wrap up and answer your question about deism: I won't deny that the thought has occurred to me from time to time. What I do think, though, is that a god that would create the kind of universe we find ourselves in would have to be very different from the anthropomorphic deities traditionally imagined by organized religion.

Most religions championed by people were obviously invented by people, and the tenets of their belief betray their origins. Their gods are just like human beings, only slightly larger. They become angry and then

---

11. Felix, *Octavius*, Chapter 29.

forgive, they show jealousy and favoritism, they can be surprised, disgusted, grieved, or dismayed, they bear grudges and love those who stroke their egos. The way most religions reflect the prejudices of their creators is all too obvious: what these people imagine to be a window through which they can see God is in truth a mirror held up to their own faces.

These kinds of gods bear no relation to the universe we find ourselves in, which is so much vaster, more ancient, and stranger than anyone's imagining. The more we learn about nature, the more we come to appreciate both its inconceivably complex and elegant harmonies, as well as its utter ruthlessness and blind unconcern for anything we might call justice. If this is the handiwork of a *being*, it must be a being utterly unlike humanity or any of the gods we've dreamed up. The poet Robinson Jeffers, who believed something similar to this, called it "the wild god of the world": a kind of impersonal natural force, indifferent to humanity, creating both astonishing beauty and horrendous suffering in equal measure.

I don't believe this personally, but I could see how someone might. I can even see a kind of logic in pagan beliefs that hold that every natural force has a conscious incarnation, and that these spirits strive and wrestle with each other. But the traditional god concept of monotheism—the idea that this world was created by infinite goodness in possession of infinite power—*that* idea, I'm sorry to say, has never struck me as anything more than a cruel joke.

ROUND 7

Philosophical Theism and Christianity, Part II

It borders incomprehensible. . . . God he says, is not in the business of awarding prizes to people who live in accordance with moral rules. You will not win any special favors from him by being virtuous. . . . He loves sinners just as much as he loves you. . . . Love is what matters, not deserving, and least of all rules. In fact, love matters about everything else. It is the ultimate reality, the true nature of existence, God. . . . The fact that there was anyone at all going around preaching things like this two thousand years ago in a desert area of the Middle East is, to say the least of it, surprising . . .[1]

—BRYAN MAGEE, *CONFESSIONS OF A PHILOSOPHER*

Adam,

Your points are thought-provoking and exude a sense of skepticism that I feel is well deserved considering the matter at hand. To take stock, I feel the philosophical case for theism is strong (you disagree, though empathize with deism), the historical basis for Christianity is strong (you really disagree!), and that Christianity has theological appeal (you agree on some points, but not on others). We also agree that all experience transcendent awe, wonder, and bliss. Where we disagree is on the implications of naturalizing the religious sense to selfish genes (not just transcendent awe, but add morality and free will)—more on that later.

1. Magee, *Confessions of a Philosopher*, 277–78.

Philosophical Theism and Christianity, Part II

For now, let's focus on Jesus Myth Theory. Though I obviously don't share your view, I've certainly considered it. Actually, it reminds me of one of my favorite books, Malcolm Gladwell's *The Tipping Point*.[2] The basic idea touches upon some of the things you mentioned. Sometimes, when the stage is set, it doesn't take much for an epidemic to spread. As relates to our discussion, we're talking about a prescientific, god-worshipping, first-century, oral tradition, Jewish-Roman era where basic record keeping was minimal—forget investigative reporting or robust scholarly debate. Like the housing boom, the market was ripe. Cue in a timely myth and it was off to the races. Then Rome got behind it—the rest was history. What if Jesus never really existed?

The truth seeker must approach this question with caution. Should one's skeptical hairs tingle equally for the Christian on the "overwhelming evidence" as they do for the atheist denying his very existence? *Absolutely*. So let's explore further. You definitely have a bone to pick with Ehrman, my friend! In your words,

> On this point he's flat-out wrong. The idea that we have as much or more historical evidence for Jesus' existence as we do for anyone else from that time period just isn't true, and he knows it.

Paging Bart Ehrman, Adam Lee is in the alley and he wants to drop the mitts. I'm a hockey guy so I'm digging your swagger, but be careful. Ehrman is a heavyweight and a leading scholar on the topic (and also happens to be an agnostic) and finds Jesus Myth Theory "so extreme and so unconvincing to 99.99 percent of the real experts that anyone holding them is as likely to get a teaching job in an established department of religion as a six-day creationist is likely to land on in a bona fide department of biology."[3]

I'm not sure why he would exaggerate or intentionally lie, but I'll attempt to provide a few points on his position (and the vast majority of non-believing scholars). Remember Ehrman's point is on the *totality of historical evidence* of Jesus' life as compared to other figures in ancient history, not the resurrection. I'm not surprised Jesus wasn't more prevalent on coins and sculptures as his ministry was completely scandalous—blasphemous

---

2. Gladwell, *The Tipping Point*
3. Ehrman, "Did Jesus Exist?," Huffingtonpost.com.

to the Jews and a strange cult to the Romans—no doubt a threat to the established order of both cultures (we both agreed on the martyrdom of Christians and efforts to contain the spread of Christianity). Jesus wasn't exactly the desired statesman or figurehead—at least until Christianity reached its "tipping point." Let's explore the totality of evidence in response to some of your points.

"To Name a Few"

There are over a dozen non-Christian sources. The ones I named are regarded as the most detailed corroborating evidence. You're dismissing what historians regard as mountains, so I have a feeling you wouldn't be too empathetic for the molehills!

Of course, some are much weaker references than others. But on the entirety of evidence, Jesus not existing just doesn't add up for historians. I personally have appreciated Gary Habermas's perspective. His is an interesting story as his PhD dissertation was on the historical study of the resurrection. The challenge was that he wasn't defending his research at a theological seminary, but Michigan State University. His dissertation was approved only under the pretense of using evidence outside the New Testament, what he terms "minimal facts."[4] In his words,

> According to this method, the chief (if not the only) historical data that could be utilized were those that passed two critical tests: 1) each datum had to be multiply attested by normal critical means, preferably from more than one angle. 2) The vast majority of critical scholars had to concede the probability of this historical fact.[5]

Secondly, your point on "only a few sources" as weak evidence is actually an argument for strength, according to Ehrman and other historians. Here's why: the overwhelming majority of Jews at the time were illiterate—oral tradition was the way, as you mentioned. With that, record keeping in ancient times was very poor. Given this backdrop—and that three Roman historians and one Jewish historian mention Jesus decades after his crucifixion—*is* very impressive evidence. It may not be impressive to you, but it's certainly impressive to historians.

---

4. Habermas, "The Minimal Facts Approach," Garyhabermas.com.
5. Habermas, "A Short Life," Garyhabermas.com.

Sources in Question

You're absolutely correct that many of the sources do not mention the historical person of Jesus, rather the acts and persecution of Christians themselves. We also agree that Tacitus and Josephus are the most specific references. But you spoke authoritatively on some "probable" and "obvious" points where I must stop and take question.

On Tacitus, you feel the probable explanation is that he "asked some Christians what they believed and wrote down what they told him." The issue here is that Tacitus was supposedly Rome's prominent historian with a strong record of historical verification.[6] He was as also a member of a priestly council that policed religious cults.[7] That being the case, it's quite *improbable* that he just interviewed a few Christian dudes.

On Josephus, you "reject the Testimonium Flavianum as the obvious forgery it is . . . ." But then I must ask: obvious to whom, Adam Lee and Jesus Myth adherents? Mainstream scholarship doesn't postulate the entire Josephus passage is a forgery. Rather, they accuse Christians of "sprucing it up." Even without the accused Christian additions it's apparent, in Mark Allan Powell's words, "Josephus obviously thought well of Jesus, regarding him as one who taught truth" and that he "respected Jesus as a 'wise man' and 'doer of startling deeds.'"[8]

In Totality

I agree with you that people die for nonsense all the time. I also agree that early church records are the best evidence for the martyrdom of the disciples. But with all the evidence available, is the best explanation that Jesus and the disciples didn't exist? I'll certainly admit that if you throw out the Gospels and all non-Christian sources, the Jesus Myth Theory would be the only credible view left on the table. But here's the problem: the overwhelming majority of irreligious historians don't do this. They add everything up, establish a set of criteria, look for corroboration, etc. Like detectives, they're simply adding up everything to establish what probably happened. Let's put Ehrman aside and consider scholar and historian John Dominic Crossan (who also rejects the divinity of Jesus) and the efforts of the Jesus Seminar.

---

6. Eddy, *The Jesus Legend*, 182–84.
7. Van Voorst, "Jesus Tradition in Classic and Jewish Writings," 2149–82.
8. Powell, *Jesus as a Figure in History*, 33.

META

Criticized by Christian scholars as a biased and liberal slashing of Jesus' life and sayings, the last thing the Jesus Seminar did was doubt his existence. In John Dominic Crossan's words, "that he was crucified is as sure as anything historical can ever be, since both Josephus and Tacitus . . . agree with the Christian accounts on at least that basic fact."[9]

Actually, the Jesus Seminar's portrait of Jesus was that he was a social prophet and faith healer—not divine, not the Son of God, just an extraordinary individual—killed for taking on the established order. Of course, to them the encounters of the "resurrected Jesus" have nonreligious explanations, but they certainly didn't deny his actual existence.[10] In historian Michael Grant's words, "no serious scholar has ventured to postulate the non-historicity of Jesus or at any rate very few, and they have not succeeded in disposing of the much stronger, indeed very abundant, evidence to the contrary."[11]

You mentioned the "consensus of necessity" and that Jesus Myth Theory "would undermine their entire field of inquiry and call into question what they'd been doing with their careers this whole time." But then I must ask: do quantum physicists undermine the entire field of physics? Academic progress is not undermined by a legitimate quest for truth. Just the opposite. Let truth reign supreme! Scientists and historians of today have every opportunity to advance their theories. If anything, the "tipping point" to deny Jesus' very existence is more than upon us in today's secular age. But the reigning sentiment, according to historians like Grant (an atheist) is that "modern critical methods fail to support the Christ myth theory . . . again and again . . . answered and annihilated by first rank scholars."[12]

We agree that for the truth seeker even Jesus' existence should be open for question, but we're far off on what the totality of evidence bears.

* * *

I remain intrigued by the three combined elements of Christianity that I previously mentioned: philosophical case for God in general (rationality of theism/experience of God), historical strength, and theological appeal. We

---

9. Crossan, *Jesus*, 45.
10. Funk, *The Gospel of Jesus*.
11. Grant, *Jesus*, 200.
12. Ibid.

can discuss more about the historicity of Jesus in general, but I'd actually be interested in hearing more about your rejection of theism in general.

I agree with your point that "most religions championed by people were obviously invented by people and the tenets of their belief betray their origins" and that "their gods are just like human beings," just more powerful. This seems to have led us both to the same question—is there "one true God"? As you said, if existence is "the handiwork of a being, it must be a being utterly unlike humanity or any of the gods we've dreamed up."

I would go even further. We should reject *any* idea of "a being" for it would ultimately just be a powerful being and cosmic designer that operates within the laws of nature. As you mentioned, such a being would ultimately be reduced to a Star Wars-esque impersonal natural force. I'm not persuaded by any idea of "a being," only the idea of Being Itself. This metaphysical conception, the God of the Philosophers, is infinitely metaphysically different than humans—Being and Goodness Itself (the ground and sustaining source of all being and goodness), the Unmoved Mover, and the Necessity of which all contingent things depend. Christianity accepts that this metaphysical conception of the God of the Philosophers is also the revealed *I AM* that entered into human history, the God blasphemous to all other monotheists.

Based on the elegance and harmony of the cosmos, you're empathetic to the idea of an impersonal god. Though ultimately unpersuaded, such a god would make sense to account for beauty and goodness, but also the evil and suffering present in the world. Just for clarification, I have two questions. First, is monotheism a "cruel joke" to you because of the problem of evil and suffering? Second, your point on the elegance and harmony of the cosmos, are you a mathematical realist? Is mathematics discovered or invented? How do we explain, what Eugene Wigner so eloquently labeled, "the unreasonable effectiveness of mathematics"?[13] Though we agree on morality being objective, we disagree on the metaphysics, specifically on ontology, so I'm curious what your position is on mathematics.

---

13. Wigner, "The Unreasonable Effectiveness of Mathematics," 1–14.

META

And the day will come when the mystical generation of Jesus, by the supreme being as his father in the womb of a virgin, will be classed with the fable of the generation of Minerva in the brain of Jupiter.

—THOMAS JEFFERSON, LETTER TO JOHN ADAMS, APRIL 1823

Andrew,

Since we've gone several rounds on the historical existence of Jesus, I don't want to prolong this, but I do have a few brief remarks. First, on Josephus and the Testimonium Flavianum. You wrote that "mainstream scholarship doesn't postulate the entire Josephus passage is a forgery, rather they accuse Christians of sprucing it up" and suggested that "even without the accused Christian additions," Josephus had a positive view of Jesus. That's what makes the whole passage more likely to be a forgery. As a faithful Jew writing under Roman patronage, Josephus had two very strong reasons to denounce anyone who founded a new religion that could be seen as a threat to the established order: because it would clash with his own orthodox beliefs, and because his masters would have imprisoned him or worse if he didn't.

Josephus's other writings bear this out. When he mentions other would-be messiahs such as Judas of Galilee or Theudas the magician, he unambiguously condemns them as frauds, deceivers, and false prophets. If Josephus had genuinely written about Jesus, he'd likewise have had no choice but to denounce him, not to speak well of him. You said it yourself: Jesus' ministry as described in the Gospels would be scandalous and blasphemous to any member of the powers that be!

Is it possible that there was *some* historical individual who bears *some* similarity to the Jesus of the Gospels, and whose life inspired the later legends? There's no way to rule that out. But there's also no particular reason to consider it more likely than the alternative, that he was a purely legendary figure from the start. (For the sake of completeness, there's a third possibility that I rarely see mentioned: that Jesus is a composite character, a literary figure created by blending together stories about the deeds and sayings of several different real people.) To your point on historical corroboration:

> Given this backdrop—and that three Roman historians and one Jewish historian mention Jesus decades after his crucifixion—is very impressive evidence.

As I said earlier, it's true that the ancient world didn't have newspapers, birth certificates, or Social Security numbers. In most cases, anonymous oral tradition and folklore is the only source of information we have. Even if Jesus had been a historical individual, there wouldn't be very much evidence for his life. But that doesn't mean we're obligated to lower our standards of proof! Rather, it means that any hypothesis about what happened in ancient history needs to be correspondingly more tentative, and our conclusions more provisional.

That's why we should be suspicious of the too-easy avowals of certainty by some of the historians you quote. When they say that no serious scholar would ever entertain the Mythical Jesus Theory, you can tell they're going well beyond what the facts support. I agree with Bart Ehrman on many issues, but on *this* issue he lashes out with a disproportionate degree of anger and defensiveness (something that's plainly visible even in the excerpt you quoted), which I think goes to show that he's being driven by an emotional attachment more than by a cool-headed and scholarly consideration of the evidence. If you call that dropping the gloves, so be it!

And, please note: even if I'm completely wrong about all of this, the only thing it would prove is that Jesus was just a human being! Even that conclusion falls far short of the Gospels, which depict him as regularly performing impossible miracles: magical exorcisms and cures, creating food out of nothing, calming storms, walking on water, resurrecting people from the dead. One Gospel goes so far as to say that when Jesus died, there was a mass resurrection of dead saints, who climbed out of their graves and walked into Jerusalem to show themselves off to the populace (Matt 27:52–53). Does it sound at all likely that something like that could have happened without creating any contemporary historical record, without even being recorded by the authors of the other gospels?

David Hume, the immortal skeptical philosopher, said it best in his *Enquiry Concerning Human Understanding,* when explaining why we should disbelieve miracle stories like these:

> The plain consequence is (and it is a general maxim worthy of our attention), "That no testimony is sufficient to establish a miracle, unless the testimony be of such a kind that its falsehood would be more miraculous than the fact which it endeavours to establish...."

> When anyone tells me that he saw a dead man restored to life, I immediately consider with myself whether it be more probable that this person should either deceive or be deceived, or that the fact which he relates should really have happened. I weigh the one miracle against the other; and according to the superiority which I discover, I pronounce my decision, and always reject the greater miracle.[14]

The closest thing we have to a contemporary source on Jesus' life is the Gospels—yet those Gospels tell utterly implausible miracle tales, which should make us treat them as unreliable sources (just as Christians are less likely to view the Muslim, Hindu, or Buddhist scriptures as being true by virtue of the implausible miracle tales that *they* contain). Just as with Josephus's Testimonium, it won't do to strip out the least believable parts and then assume that everything left over is trustworthy. In the legal system, an eyewitness who tells *some* falsehoods necessarily undermines his own credibility in other matters, and I think that's a useful principle to bring to historical analysis as well.

Moving on to mathematics, you asked:

> On the elegance and harmony of the cosmos, are you a mathematical realist? Is mathematics discovered or invented? How do we explain, what Eugene Wigner so eloquently labeled, "the unreasonable effectiveness of mathematics"?

To be honest, I don't know if I'm a mathematical realist or not. I think either answer could lead to confusion. Saying that mathematics is "discovered" implies some kind of Platonic realm that stands above the material objects mathematics is used to describe, which I don't believe. But "invented" also strikes me as the wrong word, since it implies that setting one plus one equal to two was just an arbitrary choice that someone made.

The best alternative, I think, is to say that mathematics is a language. Language was created by human beings to describe the real patterns we observe in the world around us. Mathematics serves the same purpose, just in a more formal and precise way than spoken- or written-word languages. It's not surprising that we can mathematically model a particle collision, just as it's not surprising that we can use words to describe what a sunset looks like, because that's why those languages were created.

As far as the "unreasonable" effectiveness of mathematics, I agree that mathematics is effective, but I don't know if it's unreasonably so. Scientists,

---

14. Hume, *Enquiry*, Section X, Part 1.

especially physicists, sometimes speak of some ineffable quality of beauty or elegance in their equations that often corresponds to empirical truth. And it's remarkable that elementary particles and other natural phenomena precisely follow such simple mathematical laws. (How do they *know*? Why can't some rebellious electron obey $e=mc^3$ instead?)

On the other hand, we're discovering many complex phenomena for which mathematics doesn't seem especially well-suited; where mathematical solutions, if they exist at all, are far beyond the ability of any ordinary person and can only be approximated by supercomputers. I'm thinking of chaotic, nonlinear systems like the weather, where even the tiniest variation in initial conditions grows hugely over time. Even some "pure" mathematical problems seem resistant to simple solutions, like the four-color map theorem or the densest way to stack spheres, both of which were only proven by hundreds of pages of exhaustive computer-assisted analysis.

On monotheism, you inquired:

> Is monotheism a "cruel joke" to you because of the problem of evil and suffering?

I think that's a fair way to put it. If you regard the cosmos as a created thing, and if you accept the principle that you can learn about the creator by studying the creation, you'll find it hard to avoid some disturbing conclusions. The universe is beautiful and elegant, it's true, but it's neither loving nor moral. On the contrary, it's a terrifyingly violent and chaotic place.

At the center of our galaxy there's a black hole with the mass of a billion suns, a bottomless chasm in the fabric of reality that shreds and swallows whole stars. The explosive death of massive stars seeds the cosmos with the elements of new life, but any living planet that happened to be nearby would be scoured clean by radiation. Our planet bears the scars of countless cosmic impacts, some of them vast enough to nearly eradicate life.

A little closer down to Earth, there's plenty of beautiful, elegant evil for us to train our gazes on. There's a sinister precision in the way that a virus homes in on a living cell, pierces its outer membrane, and hijacks its internal machinery, forcing it to do nothing but manufacture more and more copies of the virus, until it bursts open to release the viral particles and continue the infection. Spider webs are beautiful when they glisten in the morning dew, but to the insects that get trapped in them, they represent horrific death. Brood-parasite birds like the cuckoo lay their eggs in another bird's nest; when the cuckoo chick hatches, the first thing it does is push the other eggs out to shatter on the ground, so that the oblivious parents will devote all their attention to feeding and raising the intruder.

Charles Darwin famously wrote about the Ichneumonidae, a family of wasps that hunt caterpillars. When an ichneumonid wasp finds its prey, it delivers a precise sting, calibrated to paralyze but not kill the caterpillar, so that the wasp can drag it back to its burrow. There it lays its eggs, using the caterpillar's living body as a larder so that, when the larvae hatch, they can devour it alive. Some species put even more gruesome twists on this strategy: we recently discovered one dubbed the bone-house wasp, which lays its eggs in nests bricked up by walls of dead ants, like some insectile serial killer.

I feel a shudder when I contemplate the evil elegance of adaptations like this. Of course, from *my* perspective, I'm anthropomorphizing. I think that these species arise from the churn of evolution, and evolution is a merciless process, one that rewards survival and reproduction, not necessarily compassion. (Compassion *can* arise, in intelligent and social species like our own, where mutual cooperation is an aid to survival—but evolution can also reward strategies that, from our perspective, are horrifically cruel.)

But if you believe in a creator who takes an active role in creation, then you must believe that, in some sense, God approves of things like this. Strictly speaking, that doesn't tell us anything about whether such a god exists. But it *does* tell us a lot about whether that being would be a good source of morals; and Christianity, of course, has always insisted as an integral part of its definition that God is absolutely good.

What do you think about this? How do you reconcile belief in a moral creator with the chaotic and unjust universe we live in?

ROUND 8

A/theological and Metaphysical Puzzles, Part I

But why has our physical world revealed such extreme mathematical regularity that astronomy superhero Galileo Galilei proclaimed nature to be "a book written in the language of mathematics," and Nobel Laureate Eugene Wigner stressed the "unreasonable effectiveness of mathematics in the physical sciences" as a mystery demanding an explanation?[1]

—MAX TEGMARK, *OUR MATHEMATICAL UNIVERSE*

Adam,

You've laid out some fantastic points for discussion. Before addressing mathematical ontology and the problem of evil and suffering, I'll add some departing thoughts on Jesus.

Historicity of Jesus and Skepticism of Miracles

We've exchanged quite a bit on the historicity of Jesus! I'm unpersuaded by your view as it flies in the face of historical scholarship. To briefly address your point on Josephus, we agree a very prominent Jewish historian would *not* have penned statements such as "He was the Christ" or "if it be lawful to call him a man." As I mentioned, partial authenticity with added Christian

---

1. Tegmark, *Our Mathematical Universe*, 6.

interpolations is the overwhelming opinion among historians.[2] The consensus among scholars as to the original text is the following:

> At this time there appeared Jesus, a wise man. For he was a doer of startling deeds, a teacher of people who received the truth with pleasure. And he gained a following both among many Jews and among many of Greek origin. And when Pilate, because of an accusation made by the leading men among us, condemned him to the cross, those who had loved him previously did not cease to do so. And up until this very day the tribe of Christians (named after him) has not died out (*Ant.* 18.63–64).[3]

Throwing out the entire passage as a forgery ignores this fact as well as the logic of historians on a few key points. First, the content and style (outside the suspected Christian additions), as pointed out by Evans,[4] Vermes,[5] Van Voorst,[6] Wansbrough,[7] and Köstenberger[8] is highly suggestive of Josephus. Secondly, multiple versions of the Josephus passage have been discovered (Greek, Syrian, and Arabic) and contrasted and many scholars believe that the Arabic version contains the original Josephus passage prior to any additions.[9] Thirdly, as highlighted by Grabbe,[10] Feldman,[11] and Baras,[12] the early church father Origen wrote about Josephus mentioning Jesus (yet Josephus rejecting him as Messiah), supporting partial authenticity and that Origen had in hand the original text without interpolation.

I think the zeal you see in historians like Ehrman is akin to scientists when extreme minority views (with suspected philosophical underpinnings) are placed within mainstream scholarship. Physics, for example, is the study of matter and energy and amongst its discoveries have been the speed of light, the Big Bang, etc. The methods of physics reveal these as facts as best physics can determine. Similarly, Jesus' historical existence

2. Evans, *Jesus and His Contemporaries*, 43.
3. Dunn, *Jesus Remembered*, 141.
4. Evans, *Jesus and His Contemporaries*, 316.
5. Vermes, *Jesus in the Jewish World*, 35–43.
6. Van Voorst, *Jesus Outside the New Testament*, 89–90.
7. Wansbrough, *Jesus and the Oral Gospel Tradition*, 185.
8. Köstenberger, *The Cradle, the Cross, and the Crown*, 104–8.
9. Ibid.
10. Grabbe, "Jesus Who is Called the Christ," 61–67.
11. Feldman, "Flavius Josephus Revisited," 823.
12. Baras, "The Testimonium Flavianum and the Martyrdom of James," 340–41.

is the overwhelming mainstream view among historians. Challenging the age of the Earth for theological motivation (Young Earth Creationism for example) is met with scorn by physicists because one's theological view is being put forward to challenge the best available knowledge of the discipline. History, though it differs from physics in aim, is a truth-seeking methodological process. Historical hypotheses that meet certain criteria are granted certain historical strength. And Jesus' existence, if you value history, to return to John Dominic Crossan, "is as sure as anything historical can ever be."[13] I won't charge that naturalism is governing your view; just that Jesus Myth Theory is weak on historical grounds.

Moving past historical skepticism, you moved to philosophical skepticism and highlighted Hume, who is perhaps the most influential skeptical philosopher of all time. The signature of Hume is his extreme skeptical epistemology. If he's right, we're both in trouble, as miracles and objective morality go out the window—bye-bye theism and secular humanism. Though we ended up in different places, I think we both appreciate his perspective. Skepticism is an immensely important balance to any truth claim (miracles for empathetic theists, moral ontology for sympathetic naturalists) and should be a necessary and essential consideration for anyone who calls themselves a truth seeker. On miracles, I agree we should be skeptical and always seek out alternative explanations. As I've noted, Christianity hangs on the rationality of theism and the possibility of miracles to begin with. If theism is bunk, so is Christianity (and all religions for the matter). But if theism is possible/probable, so is the miraculous. What we're ultimately getting at here is justified belief. If the philosophical case for theism is strong, along with the historical events surrounding the Christian narrative, one will be inclined to consider if Jesus was the revealed *I AM*. Besides the historical facts you reject, most critical scholars also admit the empty tomb and the disciples' post-resurrection appearances[14] that reinvigorated the scattered and skeptical and inspired an unprecedented movement, against all odds, of which they were prepared to give their very lives.

Of course, naturalized alternatives should be considered (conspiracy theory, hallucination, etc.). As a truth seeker, I would demand nothing less. All the while, as a truth seeker, I must be willing to consider the possibility of a miracle. For this truth seeker, the miraculous is not only possible, but

---

13. Crossan, *Jesus*, 45.
14. Habermas, "The Case for Christ's Resurrection," 180–98.

probable, given theism, and that best explanation for Christianity is that Christ is God.

In short, should we doubt miracles stories? *Absolutely* (point of agreement). Is Christian theism a justified belief? *Absolutely* (point of contention).

Mathematical Realism

Back to metaphysics, on mathematics, I am very much a realist, so I'll say this: if you feel mathematics is just a language created by humans to describe patterns of the world around us—you're definitely *not*. The upshot is you're now rejecting mathematical ontology but embracing moral ontology, which certainly piques my curiosity! If abstract truths such as mathematics and morality are created by humans, how then is morality objective? I find objective, metaphysical, ontological truths such as morality and mathematics completely consistent with theism, but I must agree with philosopher Timothy Williamson and Alex Rosenberg that "finding a place for mathematics"[15] is a major problem for naturalism.[16] I don't want to rehash our discussion on morality, but I would love your thoughts on how one can reject all these spooky ontologies such as God, teleology, mathematical ontology, yet posit objective moral ontology.

That said, on the unreasonable effectiveness of mathematics, we very much disagree. To take a few lines from author and astrophysicist Mario Livio:

> Even if logic had been deeply embedded in our ancestor's brains, it is difficult to see how this ability could have led to abstract mathematical theories of the subatomic world, such as quantum mechanics, that display stupendous accuracy.... Researchers use mathematical models to product new phenomena, new particles, and the results of never-before-performed experiments and observations. What puzzled Wigner and Einstein was the incredible success of the last two processes. How it is possible that time after time physicists are able to find mathematical tools that not only explain the existing experimental and observational results, but which also lead to entirely new discernment and new predictions?[17]

---

15. Williamson, "Naturalism and Its Limits," Nytimes.com
16. Rosenberg, "Why I am a Naturalist," Nytimes.com.
17. Livio, *Is God a mathematician?*, 246–47

We certainly agree that mathematics is a language of the rational order of the world and that symbolic representations are a created language, but we break on mathematics simply being "created by humans." The symbolic representations are created, but not the underlying truths.

It's not just the amazing accuracy of mathematics; but also its predictive power. How could we create a language for something that, at the time, we have no clue empirically what we are describing? That would not be a language; it would be predicting the future. If created, mathematics' stupendous accuracy and amazing predictive power would be happy coincidence (what are the odds?), a curious situation to say the least.

Teleology, Evil, and Suffering

We agree that the universe is beautiful and elegant, yet harsh and terrifying. Remember, in my view, the entirety of nature is hylomorphic and teleological. Because there is ontology (goodness, mathematics, etc.) and ends in nature, because anything exists at all, there is a First Cause, an Unmoved Mover, and Being and Goodness Itself. Because all finite things exist in between a state of potential and actualization, there is Pure Act, the Necessity of which all contingent things depend. The hallmark of teleology is metaphysical realism for ontology and ends in nature. Matter/form, potentiality/actuality—all contingent things, including human beings, are irreducible composites of physical (matter) and immaterial ontological properties (form). The end of a human is to achieve their potential as rational animal.

From go, you can see why we differ on applied metaphysics (such as mathematics and morality), given our respective worldviews. A consequence of teleology, besides mathematical and moral realism, is also the harshness of nature. To your point that God must approve of "evil adaptations"—you're right that you are anthropomorphizing. The wasps and spiders you mentioned are merely working towards their ends, given their nature. They are not loving, moral, or rationally free creatures. They are just doing what they do, what "well-being" is for a wasp or spider. Humanity, the rational animal, on the other hand, has the potential to actualize knowledge, love, and compassion (to a finite degree of course). The term "lowlife" is actually a nice Aristotelian summary of teleology and virtue. Take a total hedonist for example—such an individual would be choosing to act as an animal—a low level of existence given one's potential as a rational animal.

With such a harsh and "unjust universe," how could God be perfectly good and the source of morality? We'd first have to start with ontology and an objective definition of goodness and justice, which is what I find lacking in a naturalistic worldview. As C. S. Lewis famously penned, "my argument against God was that the universe seemed so cruel and unjust. But how had I got this idea of just and unjust? A man does not call a line crooked unless he has some idea of a straight line. What was I comparing this universe with when I called it unjust?"[18]

Remember that this unjust nature has also resulted in not only unfathomable beauty, as you mentioned, but also conscious creatures. As agnostic Paul Davies says, "this can be no trivial detail, no minor by-product of mindless, purposeless forces. We are truly meant to be here."[19] As you know, the cosmos and all life within it exist within an incomprehensible sweet spot of necessary physical constants. Without nature being her exact way, there would be no nature or conscious humanity questioning what a just nature is.

Now, what I think you're ultimately getting at is a potentially better universe and the problem of evil and suffering. As rational and emotional creatures, I believe this to be an irresistible topic for someone considering Christianity as it touches both on rational coherence (existence of God) and whether this is a God worth loving (character of God). That said, I think William Lane Craig correctly points out the problem of evil and suffering is actually two separate problems: an "intellectual problem" and an "emotional problem."[20]

The intellectual problem is simply a matter of coherence on how the existence of evil and suffering is logically consistent with a loving God. Rationally, there is no problem. The emergence of rationally free, loving, moral, and compassionate human beings comes at quite a price—the potentiality of nature, thus the potentiality of humanity. God created a universe that resulted in the emergence of such conscious creatures with free will. On one hand, it's beautiful and quite poetic—we're offered a part in the creation process. On the other hand, nature can be quite unforgiving and freedom, by definition, requires a choice for good or evil. If my logical reply to your question was "free will," "the greater good," or perhaps the most appropriate—"I don't know"—all would be coherent. Cold comfort,

---

18. Lewis, *Mere Christianity*, 38.
19. Davies, *The Mind of God*, 232.
20. Craig, "The Problem of Evil," Reasonablefaith.org

A/theological and Metaphysical Puzzles, Part I

I realize, but certainly coherent. In the words of agnostic philosopher Paul Draper:

> In order for a logical argument from evil to succeed, it is necessary to show that, for some known fact about evil, it is logically impossible for God to have a good moral reason to permit that fact to obtain. This, however, is precisely what most philosophers nowadays believe cannot be shown.[21]

The emotional problem—now we're getting into the real challenge in trying to comprehend the character of God that would allow evil and suffering. As finitely rational, yet emotional creatures, we'll never have an answer we're fully satisfied with. "Free will," "greater good," or "I don't know" are all valid logically, but certainly not comforting. Natural disasters and the unspeakable evils committed by humanity are both horrifying. The *Why, God?* question is one that I ask myself frequently. I think most believers, if they are honest, struggle with this as well. It's quite a common theme in the Scriptures. As I said at our debate, this is the strongest issue on the table to the question of God's *character*. If we can't get an answer as to why, the question ultimately amounts to: Is this a God worth loving?

The Christian paradox is that God entered into human suffering. To take a line from Tim Keller,

> If we ask again the question, "Why does God allow evil and suffering to continue?" and we look at the cross of Jesus, we still do not know what the answer is. However, we now know what the answer isn't. It can't be that He doesn't love us. It can't be that He is indifferent or detached from our condition. God takes our misery and suffering so seriously that He was willingly to take it on Himself.[22]

If you're correct about the Jesus Myth Theory, this is quite unmoving and Christianity is just another myth to be discarded. But if there is good reason for theism and Christianity, it's deeply moving, a revelation of the character of God, yet an incomplete answer to the question *Why, God?*

What can one surmise about such a theology? First, it's philosophically coherent. It posits potentiality in nature (beauty and harshness) and humanity (good and evil). Ontologically, there is such thing as objective goodness. God, Being, Goodness, and Infinite Wisdom, has the full answer to the problem of evil and suffering. We can only grasp finitely that God,

---

21. Draper, "The Problem of Evil," 335.
22. Keller, *The Reason for God*, 30–31.

objective goodness, and free will exist, thus a "greater good" is coherent rationally. Secondly, it's emotionally unsettling. Not knowing why will always be unsettling. Thirdly, though evil and suffering are rationally coherent with a loving God, Christianity also reveals a paradox: Goodness and Being Itself entered into our suffering. *I AM*, of infinite power, was revealed—a new testament—from law to love. The leader becomes the servant. Not knowing the full answer why, we're left only with the example of Jesus.

Is this a God worth loving? Rationally, I'm hooked on the idea of God, Pure Act, Goodness and Being Itself, and the Necessity of which all contingent things depend. Emotionally, though always unsettled at not knowing why, I'm inspired by the Christian paradox and the revealed character of God.

Since we're getting deep here philosophically, what are your thoughts on consciousness? Are you more of an eliminative materialist, a functionalist, or somewhat of a naturalistic dualist? Is consciousness a meaningless word (i.e., just brain)? Is it ontologically different than brain? Is it adequately accounted for to date in your view or do you feel it's still very much a work in progress?

A/Theological and Metaphysical Puzzles, Part I

There is always a certain glamour about the idea of a nation rising up to crush an evil simply because it is wrong. Unfortunately, this can seldom be realized in real life; for the very existence of the evil usually argues a moral weakness in the very place where extraordinary moral strength is called for.[23]

—W. E. B. DU BOIS

Andrew,

We'll get into consciousness soon, but before we do, I have a few more things I want to say about the problem of evil. Let's jump right into it. You wrote:

> The emergence of rationally free, loving, moral, and compassionate human beings comes at quite a price—the potentiality of nature, thus the potentiality of humanity. God created a universe that resulted in the emergence of such conscious creatures with free will. On one hand, it's beautiful and quite poetic—we're offered a part in the creation process. On the other hand, nature can be quite unforgiving and freedom, by definition, requires a choice for good or evil.

It's a common move among theists to argue that God places supreme value on human free will, and that true free will necessitates the possibility of people misusing it to choose evil, as you've done here. So here's my request: tell me about heaven.

Will there still be natural disasters, sickness, suffering, greed, jealousy, loneliness, resentment, cruelty in heaven? If not, how can that possibly be? You just said that human freedom "by definition" results in all those evils. Is there a special, better kind of freedom in heaven that allows people the ability to choose but without the possibility of choosing wrong? If so, then why didn't God create people with *that* kind of freedom in the first place? Or do people in heaven no longer have free will—but if so, how do you square that with your claim that we need free will to be "loving, moral and compassionate" creatures rather than mere puppets dangling from strings?

This ties into a larger point, which is that in the traditional Christian conception, God creates humans with strong desires to do things he doesn't

---

23. Du Bois, *The Suppression of the African Slave-Trade*, 195.

want them to do, and then punishes them when they're unable to resist the temptations of the nature he gave them. In the New Testament, Jesus tells people not to look lustfully at a woman and not to be angry with their brother. These are the simplest and most basic emotions! You might as well punish people for being hungry or sleepy.

Human beings aren't blank slates. We have a nature and a set of dispositions which we didn't choose, and which incline us toward acting in certain kinds of ways. Sometimes, those impulses are so strong that they're literally overpowering. If God exists, it's completely nonsensical that he'd give us dispositions that were the *opposite* of what he wanted. It would be like running a gambling game with weighted dice and then punishing the other person for losing. If we had been created by a being who had moral standards he expected us to meet, why wouldn't he have given us dispositions toward good rather than evil, so that sin held no attraction for us? Does God *want* there to be evil?

You said that "the Christian paradox is that God entered into human suffering." I agree that this is a "paradox" in the sense that it doesn't explain anything at all. Imagine if you heard about an MSF doctor who traveled to Liberia during the 2014 Ebola epidemic to help people suffering from the virus. Further imagine that this doctor is so brilliant, he's invented a miraculous vaccine, which if given to an Ebola sufferer would immediately and permanently cure them. Now imagine that when he steps off the plane, he says: "Even though I have the vaccine, I'm not going to give it to you. But to prove how loving and compassionate I am, I'm going to deliberately infect myself with Ebola so that I can suffer alongside you."

I doubt you'd be inclined to accept this as proof of this doctor's benevolence. I think you'd ask, and would be well within your rights to ask: *Why*? What does that accomplish? Adding pointless and unnecessary suffering on top of more pointless and unnecessary suffering doesn't show compassion at all. Allowing people to suffer when you have the ability to help them is the act of a sadist. Choosing to share in their suffering rather than alleviate it, at most, proves that you're also a masochist!

You said that this is "philosophically coherent," but I'd argue that it's anything but. Much the contrary, I'd say that the Christian scheme is shot through with so many gaps, paradoxes, and contradictions that it's far simpler and more consistent to consider it false. Just as Copernicus's simpler, heliocentric solar system replaced the Ptolemaic earth-centered system and its proliferation of unwieldy epicycles, it's much more straightforward to conclude that the world is complete in itself and is governed by impersonal natural forces unconcerned with good or evil.

Moving on, you asked me: "Is consciousness a meaningless word (i.e., just brain)? Is it ontologically different than brain?" Now you're getting into one of my favorite topics! As with the question of mathematics, I think this is an area where labels frequently confuse rather than clarify. I'd describe my view in this way: the mind *is* what the brain *does*. Rational thought, emotion, and consciousness arise from, and are produced by, the complex patterns of information that flow along the hundreds of trillions of neural connections in our heads.

Our scientific understanding of precisely *how* the brain produces the mind is in its very earliest stages. I'm sure that people a hundred years from now will look back with amused superiority on the primitive beliefs of our era, just as we now look at people who attributed the weather to thunder gods rather than jet streams and axial tilt.

Even so, we have abundant evidence that this view is true. We already know that all the functions of consciousness are produced by specific regions within the brain, and can be altered or lost when those brain regions are damaged or impaired. Just as reprogramming a computer can change how it behaves and what it does, physical and chemical changes to the brain can "reprogram" a person's personality, wiping away the things that make you who you are, or giving you new and different character traits.

Any neuroscientist can cite countless examples of syndromes and disorders that have effects like this. I'll give just a few.

There's nothing more fundamental to the self than memory. Memory is what shapes us, what makes us who we are. It makes it possible for us to learn from our experiences, to grow and change as human beings. So what happens to the self when a person's memory ceases to function?

One of the twentieth century's best-known cases was a British musician named Clive Wearing, who contracted a severe case of viral encephalitis. He survived, but the disease destroyed his hippocampi, two seahorse-shaped brain regions known to be critical for the formation of memory. As a result, he lost the ability to form any new memories—meaning that his life has contracted to the span of short-term memory, perhaps thirty seconds or less. Beyond that brief window, everything he sees and hears is lost.

Wearing's amnesia is so severe that he continually believes he's only just awoken from unconsciousness. He can and does read the same book or watch the same show over and over, and is just as surprised by the outcome every time. He fills diaries with the same lines, repeated endlessly: "Now I am completely awake, for the first time in years." Whenever he sees his wife Deborah, he greets her with a rush of joy and relief, declaring that it's been ages since they were together—even if she only stepped out of the room for a few minutes.

The cruelest irony of all is that Wearing doesn't know, and can't be made aware of, what it is that's wrong with him. As the neurologist Oliver Sacks wrote, "He was acutely, continually, agonizingly conscious that something bizarre, something awful, was the matter"[24]—but that's the most he can ever understand. He can't learn the nature of his condition any more than he can learn any other new information. Barring some radical advance in medical science, he'll be this way for the rest of his life.

Does this fit with a non-materialist theory of the self? If the mind is something more than the brain, how is it possible that a person can learn and grasp some new piece of information one moment, then have it completely slip from his consciousness the next?

Brain disorders can affect personality as well as memory. There's an ailment variously called Pick's disease or frontotemporal dementia. It's a rare degenerative condition that's similar to Alzheimer's, except that instead of attacking the memory, it affects the brain's frontal lobes, which are the seat of "executive" mental functions like long-term planning, judgment, and impulse control.

The early symptoms include loss of empathy, inconsiderate or tactless behavior, uncontrollable aggression, and poor impulse control. It can give rise to compulsive behavior like binge eating, hoarding, pathological lying, inappropriate sexual acts like public masturbation, or petty crimes like running red lights or shoplifting. It's not uncommon for sufferers to suddenly give up political or religious convictions they'd held all their lives. In one case I've read about, a woman with late-stage FTD who'd been a lifelong Lutheran spontaneously converted to Roman Catholicism and claimed to be in love with her priest.[25] Other sufferers have been known to unexpectedly abandon spouses and families.

Lastly, there are brain disorders that alter behavior. Another strange syndrome is called akinetic mutism. It often results from damage to a part of the brain called the anterior cingulate cortex, which is thought to be where systems of attention, emotion, and short-term memory come

---

24. Sacks, "The Abyss," NewYorker.com
25. Miller, "Neuroanatomy of the Self," 817–21.

together. People with this disorder are awake, conscious, and aware, but won't move or speak. Their eyes track moving objects, but their faces are blank and passive. Occasionally they can be coaxed to give monosyllabic answers to questions, but usually they won't respond to anything, even a painful stimulus like a pinprick.

This isn't always a permanent condition; people have been known to recover from it. And if you ask them what it was like, they'll usually say that they remember everything perfectly well. They'll insist that they weren't in pain or paralyzed, just that they had no desire to say or do anything. It's as if their will was shut off, like flicking a switch.

Under a materialist explanation of the mind, the existence of these disorders isn't surprising. The traits that make us who we are come from the brain, and when the brain is damaged or reduced in function, the workings of the mind are changed as well. There's no self that's separate from the wiring of your neurons. But if consciousness, personality, and free will are the gifts of an immaterial soul, it's very difficult, if not impossible, to explain how they can be arbitrarily altered or effaced by physical injury to the brain.

After all, Christians are wont to believe that the *total destruction* of the brain upon bodily death doesn't have any effect on one's consciousness! How, then, is it possible that much lesser damage to the brain can result in such profound changes? And if you incur brain trauma that changes your personality, then which self is the "real" you, the one before the brain damage, or after?

ROUND 9

A/theological and Metaphysical Puzzles, Part II

There is perhaps no other phenomenon besides consciousness that is so familiar to each of us and yet has been so elusive to any systematic study, philosophical or scientific. In thinking about consciousness, the puzzlement one often finds oneself in is rather like St. Augustine's riddle in his contemplations about the nature of time: When no one asked him, he knew what it was; being asked, however, he no longer did.[1]

— GÜVEN GÜZELDERE,
   "THE MANY FACES OF CONSCIOUSNESS"

Adam,

Thanks so much for your eloquent reply. The character of God, heaven, free will, the problem of evil and suffering, consciousness ... deep my friend, deep. Let's get right to it!

Free Will

We agree that humans are not blank slates and that free will is a hallmark of philosophical theism. I have metaphysical beef with Platonic conceptions of theism as well as Democritus's materialism (more on that later) which is why I'm attracted to hylomorphism and teleology, potentiality, actuality,

1. Güzeldere, "The Many Faces of Consciousness," 1.

A/theological and Metaphysical Puzzles, Part II

ends in nature, and humanity as the rationally free animal. With a teleological worldview, it follows necessarily that humans carry immense potential for both good and evil. Nevertheless, it would be difficult to throw stones at just one end of our nature (physical inclinations) without considering it in totality (freedom, rationality, love).

Consider sexual attraction for example. While we may have a physical inclination towards "lust" (seeing another person as merely a physical object), it can be rationally counterbalanced towards a committed relationship *beyond* just lust. Same with anger. Letting lust and anger rule one's life is a low level of existence, given our nature. To your question on Jesus' teachings, I believe teleology and virtue is at the heart of the matter, reaching one's potential as a rational animal, as opposed to being a "slave to the flesh."

To your follow up question on why God wouldn't "have given us dispositions toward good rather than evil, so that sin held no attraction for us?"—this is just a restatement of the problem of evil. I'll come back to that in a moment but for now let's say that God created us as perfect "love robots." We now must ask ourselves the timeless question posed by Bob Marley, Whitesnake, and Survivor: "Is this Love?" My answer is no.

This all goes back to freedom and potentiality. Human freedom is ultimately human potentiality (for good and evil) and love is the ultimate expression of freedom, as is hate. If there is a God, which I contend there is, then sin holding "no attraction to us" is simply preprogrammed determinism—not freedom, transcendence, or love.

"Tell me about heaven" you asked, but you have to understand what I believe this phrase equates to: *tell me about the indescribable and being in the presence of God*. By definition, I can't, my friend! Is there a special kind of freedom in heaven? Again, this is way beyond my epistemological pay grade. If you're asking me to speculate whether in heaven there is no capacity to sin or in the presence of God sin is not chosen, my answer would be that I don't know. I think what you may have been implying is another question: why have any sin or suffering at all? Why didn't we all just wake up in heaven? That is a fantastic question, one that I've wondered myself. Again, my answer would be that I don't know. I can only postulate that it has something to do with freedom and love being the ultimate expression of freedom.

I commend the depth of your questions. With the problem of evil and suffering, I think the intellectual and emotional problems are frequently conflated, which is unsurprising given our intellectual and emotional selves. As I said earlier, I maintain that the logical problem of evil and suffering is quite weak. If you consider the two positions, "I don't understand unanswered scientific questions, thus God exists" and "I don't understand why God would allow X, thus there is no God"—both are equally invalid.

With Christianity, my point wasn't that I understand the entirety of God's nature, the Trinity, or the "greater good." Just the opposite. I think this is evidenced by your "Ebola Doctor" thought experiment. *I can't comprehend why someone would do such a thing*—fair enough. *I can't imagine why God would do such a thing (enter into human existence and die for all of humanity)*—should you be able to fully comprehend it? The question is whether or not God exists and if Jesus is God. If Christianity is true, it will ultimately surpass your comprehension. As you know, something beyond comprehension is not logically incoherent.

As much as we agree that the Christian story is paradoxical, we differ in it having no information to offer. If Christianity is true, as Keller highlighted, the answer isn't that God doesn't care. The *I AM* and giver of all existence entered into it to idealize the ultimate end of humanity: to love and serve others. The life and ministry of Jesus reveals the character of God. The Christian narrative also reveals something about free will. God will not force love on anyone. This logically addresses why God didn't create love robots or doesn't intervene all the time to prevent evil. As J. L. Mackie highlights, "we can concede that the problem of evil does not, after all, show that the central doctrines of theism are logically inconsistent with one another. But whether this offers a real solution of the problem is another question."[2] What I think you, Mackie, and I agree on is the emotional problem. Personally, I think the heart of the matter lies not with evil, but natural suffering. Why wouldn't God stop or at least minimize natural suffering? For me, this has been and will continue to be a lifelong relational and emotional issue. The "greater good" answer is valid logically, but will always press emotionally. *Why, God?* will always be a question for believers.

Before we turn the page to consciousness, I'm curious how you wrestle with the topic of free will. Your metaphysical hero Democritus is the face of determinism who maintained that there are no final and formal causes, "only atoms and void" controlled by causal laws. And I'm not just picking on you: any deterministic worldview—Democritian materialism, Watchmaker

---

2. Mackie, *The Miracle of Theism*, 154.

deism, or predestination theology—all must face the music that we're either selfish genes or God-controlled memes.

As I've mentioned, the hallmark of hylomorphism and teleology is an ontological realism of potentiality and actuality. God, Pure Act, Being and Goodness Itself, guarantees objective goodness ontologically, as well as potentiality in nature (potential for the rationally free animal to reach that end). Again, I understand the appeal of naturalism. I'm also immensely attracted to secular humanism practically (again, I love the marketing, just not the metaphysics). At the same time, one must be a consistent metaphysician (at least if they care to be coherent philosophically). Going back to Dawkins, if naturalism is true ours would simply be a "universe of electrons and selfish genes, blind physical forces and genetic replication. . . . No purpose, no evil and no good. Nothing but blind pitiless indifference. . . . DNA neither knows nor cares. DNA just is, and we dance to its music."[3] This is just a contemporary restatement of Democritus, that it's all just matter and motion. As a result, many naturalists like Alex Rosenberg, Jerry Coyne, and Peter Singer throw the ontological baby out with the bathwater, holding that naturalism requires rejecting odd metaphysical entities like free will, purpose, meaning, objective morality, etc.

My issue with secular humanism is that I feel it betrays the metaphysics of naturalism. If I were a naturalist, I would agree with these thinkers that selfish genes dancing to DNA kills the idea of objective morality and free will. From Democritus to Dawkins, if everything is determined by matter and motion, how do you define/affirm/reject the idea of free will? On to a related topic . . .

Consciousness

Consciousness is one of my favorite topics as well! From your comments, I gather you're a physicalist (there is no mind/body distinction), but I'm unclear on what exactly you'd like to do with consciousness. In your words,

> Our scientific understanding of precisely how the brain produces the mind is in its very earliest stages, and I'm sure that people a hundred years from now will look back with amused superiority on the primitive beliefs of our era. . . . Even so, we already have abundant evidence that this view is true. We already know that all the functions of consciousness are produced by specific regions

3. Dawkins, *River Out of Eden*, 133.

within the brain, and can be altered or destroyed when those brain regions are damaged or impaired.

Before I grant that Adam Lee has solved the mind-body problem, I'd love to pick your brain (pardon the pun)! We certainly agree that we're growing leaps and bounds in our understanding of neuroscience. But a "scientific understanding of precisely how brain produces mind" and "abundant evidence that this view is true" is quite hasty. Allow me a few words to expand upon our discussion.

First, a "scientific understanding of how brain produces mind" is not a scientific understanding, but a philosophical one. Understanding neuroscience is separate from metaphysics, causation, and the mind-body problem. Needing more time to understand neuroscience to show "there is no mind, only brain" is, in the words of philosopher Edward Feser, "to confuse *causal correlation* for either *identity* or *supervenience*..." Feser continues:

> The reasons have had to do with certain philosophical theories about causation, not ignorance of neuroscience. The debate is rather about whether mental processes can plausibly be said to be either identical with neuronal processes or metaphysically supervenient upon them. Further discoveries in neuroscience are largely irrelevant to the question, for it is ultimately a philosophical one that requires philosophical analysis.[4]

This speaks to what atheist philosopher of science Massimo Piggliucci labels as the "crucial distinction between methodological naturalism and philosophical naturalism."[5] A related issue would be evolution and God's existence. Saying we need more time to understand the human genome to support naturalism is simply conflating methodological naturalism with philosophical naturalism. As relates to our discussion, many theists are in complete acceptance of evolution (and quite frustrated by their Intelligent Design/Creationism counterparts) and many atheists are completely against physicalism of mind (and quite frustrated by their physicalist/eliminative materialistic counterparts).

You stated that "we already know that all the functions of consciousness are produced by specific regions within the brain, and can be altered or lost when those brain regions are damaged or impaired." If we accept

---

4. Feser, *Philosophy of Mind*, 243.
5. Pigliucci, "Science and Fundamentalism," 1107.

"consciousness" as you've defined it (cognition, memory, behavior, etc.), you're absolutely right!

But here's the problem. Highlighting brain regions and functions for cognition (memory, judgement, speech, etc.) is simply uncontested neuroscience, not reasoned support for physicalism. In doing so, you've conflated brain with mind, assumed physicalism from go, and completely ignored the "mind-body problem" and what prominent philosophers of mind such as David Chalmers define as the "hard problems of consciousness."[6] These are what Chalmers labels "qualia"—the subjective, first-person, inner character of "mental" concepts that are irreducible to the physical. The question that plagues a theory such as yours is how could one physically reduce inner, subjective, firsthand experience?

By way of example, let's consider Thomas Nagel's "What It's Like to Be a Bat."[7] Nagel argues for the "subjective character of experience" and how physicalism fails to account for this phenomenon. We can't know what it's like to be a bat because we could never experience that sensory perception with sonar firsthand. Sonar experience is only apparent to a bat and thus cannot be reduced. If everything can be reduced physically, then how can one describe unique, first-person, subjective experience?

At the heart of the mind-body problem lies an ontological distinction between physical facts (objective, reducible) and mental facts (subjective, irreducible). As stated by Nobel Prize winner and quantum mechanics pioneer Erwin Schrödinger:

> The sensation of colour cannot be accounted for by the physicist's objective picture of light-waves. Could the physiologist account for it, if he had fuller knowledge than he has of the processes in the retina and the nervous processes set up by them in the optical nerve bundles and in the brain? I do not think so. We could at best attain to an objective knowledge of what nerve fibres are excited and in what proportion, perhaps even to know exactly the processes they product in certain brain cells—whenever your mind registers the sensation of yellow.... But even such intimate knowledge would not tell us anything about the sensation of colour.[8]

A hallmark of mind is "intentionality," in the words of Franz Brentano, the "intentional in-existence, the reference to something as an object, is a

---

6. Chalmers, "Facing Up to the Problem of Consciousness," 200–19.
7. Nagel, "What Is It Like to Be a Bat?," 435–50.
8. Schrödinger, *What is Life?*, 154–55.

distinguishing characteristic of all mental phenomena. No physical phenomenon exhibits anything similar."[9]

You wrote about brain function and memory, how damage to the brain results in damages to the self, and that "under a materialistic explanation of mind, the existence of these disorders isn't surprising." These things aren't surprising for any theory of mind, even for traditional dualists (of the Platonic sort who posit mind/brain as separate immaterial/material substances). Physiology is physiology. People who reject physicalism are not scientific holdouts; they just feel that physicalism doesn't address the irreducibility of consciousness. Several leading philosophers of mind such as Chalmers, Searle, and Nagel are naturalists, but do not feel mind (again, the subjective, "aboutness") is just brain.

I'm digging your enthusiasm for neuroscience—I share it! I'm also digging your rejection of Cartesian dualism—immaterial mind separate from body (what Gilbert Ryle famously labeled a "ghost in the machine")[10]—I share that as well! What I'm not digging is physicalism as a satisfactory account of mind. As you might expect my theory of mind stems from hylomorphism and teleology. This is at odds with both physicalism and dualism. On a hylomorphic view, it's not just humans but everything in nature that is an irreducible composite of matter and form. There is immaterial ontology *in* nature. Conscious humanity is the rational animal, not "just brain" (physicalism) and not an immaterial entity separate from the body (dualism).

On the "hard problems," "qualia," and intentionality—I recall from our Harrisburg debate that you were empathetic to consciousness being quite mysterious. With that, in Round Four, you mentioned that happiness is a quale—"an irreducible, first-person mental state"—which is much closer to Chalmers' "dualistic naturalism,"[11] but this would admit consciousness is irreducible to just brain. For clarification, when you stated "mind is what the brain does," did you just mean that further empirical discoveries will reduce consciousness to physical facts?

---

9. Brentano and Crane, *Psychology from an Empirical Standpoint*, 102.
10. Ryle, *The Concept of Mind*, 35.
11. Chalmers, "Facing Up to the Problem of Consciousness," 200–19.

A/theological and Metaphysical Puzzles, Part II

We know the insect decides who to eat, who to run away from, who to find sexually attractive. On the inside, within its tiny brain, does it have no perception of making choices, no awareness of its own existence? Not a milligram's worth of self-consciousness? Not a hint of a hope for the future? Not even a little satisfaction at a day's work well done? If its brain is one millionth the mass of ours, shall we deny it one millionth of our feelings and our consciousness? And if, after carefully weighing such matters, we insist it is still "only" a robot, how sure are we that this judgment does not apply as well to us?[12]

—CARL SAGAN AND ANN DRUYAN, *SHADOWS OF FORGOTTEN ANCESTORS*

Andrew,

Just to briefly return to our previous topic, on heaven and the problem of evil: If you say you don't know why God does or doesn't do X, that's fine. But in that case, you can't also say that God is good, or that his actions advance a greater good that we can't perceive. Saying that someone is good requires *some* understanding of their intentions. If you don't know why God permits evil and disaster to go unchecked, then to be consistent, you'd have to say that you don't know whether God is good or not. If he could be a good being permitting evil for his own mysterious reasons, then logically he could also be an evil being permitting good for his own mysterious reasons.

Not to pick on you here, but this is something I see from Christians a lot. When they believe God has done something that benefits them—for example, a Christian recovers for an illness after they pray for healing—they don't hesitate to declare it a miracle and an example of God's mercy and benevolence. But when something happens that harms people—say, a hurricane devastates a coastal town, or a beloved member of the church dies in a car crash—they say that we can't understand the mind of God and we have no right to judge him. Well, which is it?

On the topic of human nature and the desire to sin, let me raise one further point. You said that if we could rid ourselves of the disposition to be unloving, then the love we felt wouldn't be genuine; that we have to

---

12. Sagan and Druyan, *Shadows of Forgotten Ancestors*, 167.

choose to transcend the darker parts of our nature. In that case, let me pose this question: Does God also have dispositions to be selfish, unfaithful, and spiteful that he has to constantly struggle against? If not, does that mean his love isn't "real" either?

The Bible, for example, says that it's impossible for God to lie (Heb 6:18). Does this mean, to use your phrase, that God is a "preprogrammed computer," lacking the option to lie and deceive that's necessary for true freedom? If the ability to have done otherwise is a necessary part of moral responsibility (which I don't believe, for the record), then it seems to me that a Christian has no choice but to conclude that God isn't a moral being, but a sort of divine automaton.

This ties nicely into the question you asked about free will. This is one of those areas where I believe that philosophy has to bow to scientific evidence. We know that our brains are complex networks of neurons that communicate through electrochemical signals. If anyone asks, I'm happy to concede that yes, we humans are made of atoms moving and interacting in accordance with physical laws. I don't see how anyone can doubt that. In particular, we know that even slight changes in *which* atoms enter your body have profound effects on your psychology.

The element lithium, if taken as a drug, evens out the mood swings of manic depression. Towns that have natural lithium in their groundwater have lower rates of crime and suicide. People, especially children, who are poisoned by lead atoms from gasoline or paint become more aggressive, violent, and impulsive. A lack of iodine atoms in your diet causes lethargy, depression, and intellectual disability, which is why we add them to salt.

And those are just basic elements. As you move up the scale of complexity, there are molecules that have even more profound and subtle effects on how we think and feel. The right molecules can make us alert or sleepy, can tranquilize us or make us belligerent, can aid concentration or lower inhibitions, can erase memory or improve it, can make us see or hear things that aren't there or can banish those phantoms.

All this goes to show that our personalities, our basic selves, arise out of chemistry. We're not set apart from the universe, we're not immaterial loci of consciousness inhabiting material bodies. We *are* our bodies. We're part of the Democritean dance just like everything else.

Some might see this as demeaning or reductive, but I take the opposite view. I think atoms must be amazing if they can give rise to creatures as complex, intelligent, and adaptable as us. Besides, this view doesn't rob us

A/theological and Metaphysical Puzzles, Part II

of anything that makes us special or makes our existence meaningful. It *couldn't*. Our capacity for love, for generosity, for courage, for curiosity, for everything that makes us human—those are all real. They don't go away just because we know more about what causes them.

There's a further concern I often hear when I discuss matters of free will. As I said, our brains are made of atoms that move and interact in accordance with mathematical laws. Does this mean that a super-powerful Cartesian demon, who knows the initial state of the universe down to the subatomic level and all the physical laws that govern its subsequent evolution, could "unmask" us as deterministic robots by predicting our decisions down to the smallest detail?

Well, no. I'm happy to report that this philosopher's fear is impossible, because as we now know, atoms move and interact in *fundamentally* unpredictable ways. (In fact, Democritus correctly guessed this when he hypothesized that atoms could sometimes exhibit "random swerves.") When you have collections of billions and trillions of atoms, they collectively obey statistical laws, but on the level of a nerve synapse, where you need to understand individual molecules, that's not good enough for certainty.

This means that the laws of physics give rise to an irreducible nondeterminism in our choices. No matter how much knowledge you have about the universe, you can never build a "prediction machine" that takes a person's observed behavior as input and infallibly spits out what they're going to do next. No matter how much you know about a person's genetic makeup, upbringing, past choices, or character, there's always the potential for them to surprise you.

It sets up a false dilemma to contrast "My choices are determined by me" against "My choices are determined by a set of complicated atomic interactions." Those aren't two different answers. We *are*, each of us, a set of complicated atomic interactions. Those are just two different ways of describing the same thing. I'll gladly acknowledge that we're all part of the causal mesh of the universe. A philosophical materialist like me could hardly deny this. But that doesn't deprive us of agency.

We all owe our selves to an incomprehensibly complex causal chain, partaking of heredity, upbringing, environment, and—most important— your own earlier self. For anyone older than an infant, the choices you've made in the past are among the causal influences on you in the present. And those choices are themselves influenced by earlier choices that shaped your character, which are influenced by still earlier choices, and so on and so on. It's like water running downhill, carving channels into the landscape on its way to the sea: forming a unique pattern for everyone, yet making some courses of action more thinkable than others.

You may have heard Albert Einstein's theory of general relativity, the keystone in our understanding of gravity, summarized in this way: "Matter tells space how to curve; space tells matter how to move." I say something similar about free will: We choose what we choose because of who we are; we are who we are because of what we choose. I don't view this conclusion as having to "face the music" or otherwise swallow something unpalatable. Rather, I think it's another opportunity to learn more about the kind of beings we are, to truly know ourselves. And that's an opportunity I always welcome.

That doesn't mean there are no questions left to answer. And I'm certainly not saying that consciousness is a solved problem and all that's left is nailing down a few of the fine details. To the contrary, I believe consciousness is profoundly strange and mysterious. How could anyone claim any differently?

But I'm not taking the position that consciousness is *intrinsically* mysterious, or that it can *never* be explained. What I'm saying is that we simply don't know.

In fact, I don't think we even know enough to frame the question correctly. If a question seems unanswerable the way it's posed—like "How does the release of chemical signals by neurons give rise to qualia possessing a subjective character of experience?"—that's often a sign that we're not thinking about the problem in the right way. It may be that we don't have the right conceptual framework to approach it in a way that would lead to greater understanding. How would you explain to a medieval alchemist that no mixture of other elements would create gold, without using words like "atom" or "periodic table" that he wouldn't understand?

Another analogy I heard recently is that we understand the brain at the same level as an alien astronaut would understand our planet by looking down on it from orbit. That astronaut could see structure and change on the largest scale—the outlines of continents and seas, the shifting patterns of weather—but the much smaller, vastly more intricate details of the biosphere and human civilization would be invisible.

Just the same way, we have a basic understanding of the large-scale architecture of the brain. We know in a general sense which regions are responsible for which functions, and we can map different patterns of activity

A/theological and Metaphysical Puzzles, Part II

across the whole brain and get a broad idea of how these relate to the content of consciousness. But we don't know anything about all the complexity that resides at lower levels. We don't yet have the detailed, neuron-by-neuron-level understanding of how the brain processes information (the so-called "connectome") that I think we would need to begin asking the right questions about how the mind works.

And make no mistake, it's not remotely surprising that we don't understand this yet! The human brain is, literally, the most complex thing in the known universe. Trying to understand *how* it creates consciousness is and will be the greatest scientific undertaking that human beings have ever embarked on. We've only just taken the first few steps.

The one thing I want to emphasize is that adding a supernatural soul to the equation, or saying that consciousness isn't reducible to physics, is in no way a superior alternative to naturalism. In fact, that's just a declaration that the problem is unsolvable and there's no point studying it any further. I don't accept that defeatist notion. So far in human history, many other problems that were declared to be unsolvable have yielded to science. (You *can* create gold from other elements in a particle accelerator—just not economically!) Given that long track record of success, combined with how much we still don't know about the brain, I say it's far too early for pessimism.

Intentionality, at least, is an easy one. Intentionality exists in any complex system that has a goal (whether it's a consciously understood goal or not) and acts to overcome obstacles to that goal. Volcanoes or thunderstorms don't have intentionality because they're not *trying* to do anything; they don't change tactics to get around obstacles like mountain ranges or catch basins. To put it another way, you have intentionality when you have complex systems of matter that are arranged such that a change in the external world produces a corresponding change of behavior in the system in question.

Intentionality is abundant in the living world. Even a bacterium or an amoeba, which I think we can agree are fully reducible to assemblages of molecules, exhibit primitive forms of intentionality—pursuing tasty food, adopting various strategies to escape or hide from predators. As we move up the ladder of complexity, we find successively more sophisticated forms of intentionality: plants that grow toward the light, marine sea slugs that can learn through Pavlovian conditioning, houseflies that dodge the swatter, honeybees that dance to convey information to the hive, birds that pretend to be injured to draw predators away from their nests, elephants that mourn their dead, and animals like chimpanzees, dolphins, parrots, and crows that exhibit a basic capacity for self-recognition, abstract thought, tool use, and even language.

The closer you look, the more you see that there's no chasm of discontinuity separating human minds from other animals' minds, merely a spectrum of lesser or greater complexity. Our inner lives may be richer and more abstract, but this is a difference of degree, not kind. If you accept that animals' minds are reducible to the functioning of their brains, there seems to be little ground to argue that the same isn't also true of humans.

Is there a point in the hierarchy of minds where you'd draw the line and argue that something more than just physics is going on? If so, where is it?

ROUND 10

A/theological and Metaphysical Puzzles, Part III

From these facts one might think that the only cause is the so-called material cause; but as men thus advanced, the very facts opened the way for them and joined in forcing them to investigate the subject. . . . Why does this happen and what is the cause?

—ARISTOTLE, *METAPHYSICS, BOOK 1*

Adam,

After much of our discussion on God's existence, morality, mathematics, the problem of evil and suffering, free will, and consciousness, it's clear that metaphysics continues to be the root of our impasse. You feel that "we're part of the Democritean dance just like everything else." Sorry, bud, I have to disagree! We're part of the Aristotelian dance, which is why anything exists at all, how morality is objective, how free will exists (in any meaningful sense), why mathematics is so applicable and effective, etc. *Wink wink, nudge nudge.* Allow me to take a step back first to address some of your points, then close with some thoughts on our respective metaphysical lenses, free will, and consciousness.

God, the Problem of Evil and Suffering, and Free Will

To your point, "saying that someone is good (or evil) requires some understanding of their intentions"—I would agree. When I said I don't know, I was not saying that I have no clue, rather that God's infinite knowledge, goodness, and love is way beyond my comprehension. Nevertheless, I believe to have *some understanding* of human freedom, love as an expression of freedom, and the idea of a "greater good." Along these lines, I have some knowledge of God's love as revealed in the Christian paradigm, though the entirety surpasses my understanding.

You brought up a fantastic point that if God is "a good being permitting evil for his own mysterious reasons, then logically he could also be an evil being permitting good for his own mysterious reasons." This would be absolutely true for a deistic puppet master—a being that hovers above the clouds in a white robe pulling the strings. A watchmaker god not only opens up this possibility, but also that the clock is set according to the divine plan (potentially an evil plan). Perhaps there is an evil being and we have no free will?

The good news is we're both atheists for that god, my friend! Asking "Who created god?" or trying to separate goodness from God are fantastic questions for a powerful being, a *god*, but completely irrelevant to *God*. To Aristotle, Aquinas, and classical theists, God is Pure Act, the Necessity of which all contingent things depend, Being and Goodness Itself—being and goodness are inseparable from His nature. If you recall from our back and forth on morality, "good," in an Aristotelian-Thomistic view, is simply "well-being." In this conception, being and goodness are inseparable concepts. Because there is being and goodness in nature, there is a Source (Being and Goodness). Thus, asking "What if Pure Act (Infinite Being and Infinite Goodness) is actually bad?" is nonsensical. The necessary truths of God's nature are similar to other necessary truths such as the nature of a triangle. Trying to separate goodness from God, in the classical conception, is like trying to ask "what if $2+2=5$?"

This would address your point on free will and God's impossibility to be anything but perfection. Christians, you maintained, must conclude God is a "divine automaton" because he can't choose evil. It's true that any *being* without free will cannot have genuine love. A key point though: *God is Being Itself, not a contingent being (existing in a state between potentiality and actuality)*. God, Pure Act, is the One existing in perfect actuality and goodness. Does this mean He has no free will and His goodness isn't genuine? No, it means God is Infinite Goodness by His very nature. *Does this mean God's nature is infinitely different than ours?* Absolutely.

In an Aristotelian dance, God gives existence to all contingent things (which are a composite of matter and form). These contingent beings exist in between potentiality and actuality, pursuing certain ends, given their nature. A few of these beings; humans, the rational animal, have agency—the ability to freely and consciously pursue rational ends. It is only through formal and final causes *in* nature (back to the Aristotelian dance) that free will is even possible. It's off the cards in a materialistic Democritian dance. Back to the metaphysics . . .

Metaphysical Lenses

For Democritus, the ultimate nature of reality is "only atoms and the void"—matter and motion (material and efficient causes). For Aristotle, there are material, efficient, formal, and final causes. Nature is an irreducible composite of matter and form, all things existent in between a state of actuality and potentiality, and there are ends *in nature*. Naturally, the big questions we've been discussing are ultimately considered through our respective metaphysical lenses, so we can only do our best to square our views for coherence and consistency, and ultimately appeal to the best explanation. We agree on the rejection of Plato's dualism (Forms in an immaterial realm *separate* from nature). We also agree that matter and motion are obvious facets of reality—we differ on those being the entirety.

You've suggested consciousness and free will are areas where "philosophy has to bow to scientific evidence." Just a point of contention—for a truth seeker, it's never science vs. philosophy. Philosophy is the love of wisdom and celebration of reason, so ignoring scientific facts is simply ignoring truth, which good philosophy cannot allow. Besides an interest in philosophy, by now you've seen I'm an enthusiast for physics, biology, and neuroscience (all science for that matter—I'm a biomedical engineer by trade). How could anyone have qualms that "our brains are complex networks of neurons that communicate through electrochemical signals" (your words) and that slight changes in brain chemistry can have profound psychological effects? Never did I suggest that we are ghosts in the skull violating the laws of physics with the possession of our neurons. Same with your point on animals and humans having immense cognitive similarities. Ignoring these facts is simply ignoring science, not to mention basic common sense. Good philosophy, and a reasoned worldview, has to incorporate good science and good metaphysics.

My beef with materialism is the metaphysics. Consider your question: "is there a point in the hierarchy of minds where you'd draw the line and argue that something more than just physics is going on?" *By Aristotle's hylomorphism, I hold there is more than physics going on with everything in nature.* Consciousness and free will (on the hylomorphic view) isn't suddenly something different and spooky in the sense of the Cartesian dualism you're attacking. Descartes's horse is dead and I'd be glad to keep beating it alongside you. On the philosophical far-out-ness of a dualistic view of nature and humanity—we stand together. Dualism has immense philosophical problems.

But so does materialism. Rejecting teleology, ends in nature, and formal and final causes *inherently* creates profound philosophical problems. If you remember from our discussion on morality, I presented key philosophical arguments from atheistic thinkers who feel materialism is the worst metaphysical door to knock on for moral objectivity. I don't understand how a universe with no purpose (more on that in a moment) results in *objective* purpose. Ours would simply be a purposeless universe that has resulted in selfish genetic machines through blind variation, mutation, and selection (matter and motion).

For me, the philosophical problems for materialism are too much to bear—not because I feel it's degrading to existence, personhood, consciousness, agency, morality, and free will (I argue that it is, but that's beside the point)—it's that I feel materialism isn't true. With the big questions, if I felt Democritus's materialism (or Plato's dualism) was the best explanation, I would bite the bullet and follow the truth where it led. So I'll just add some concluding thoughts on why I think Aristotle's metaphysics is more robust as well as what I think biting the materialistic bullet philosophically entails.

Materialism and Free Will

On materialism, what does "free will" amount to? I love your enthusiasm for quantum mechanics, but a few words of caution on hanging your hat there for free will. First, quantum indeterminacy doesn't rule out determinism. *The quantum wave function described by the Schrödinger equation is deterministic.* It's only where the "measurement problem" comes in, where, in physicist Sean Carroll's words, "we are unable to deterministically predict what this outcome will be" and only then do "opinions become split about whether loss of determinism is real, or merely apparent."[1] There is where the different interpretations of quantum mechanics come in (Copenhagen, Many Worlds, etc.), which goes beyond the scope of our discussion.

What is extremely relevant to our discussion, however, is that even if quantum mechanics is truly non-deterministic, inability to predict says nothing about genuine free choice. Not knowing what an electron will do at the quantum level, as Carroll notes, is "utterly irrelevant for questions of free will."[2] The big question I was getting at is a metaphysical one: *can one have genuine free choice if everything is governed by the laws of physics (whether or not quantum mechanics is deterministic)?* This is where many naturalist scientists and philosophers chime in that free will is an illusion (Stephen Hawking,[3] Lawrence Krauss,[4] Alex Rosenberg,[5] Jerry Coyne,[6] Sam Harris[7])—that attempts to preserve free will are, in Harris's words, "theological"—a religious special plea of "not allowing the laws of nature to strip us of a cherished illusion."[8] I applaud you in trying to preserve some definition of free will, but I'm not clear as to it amounting to anything but illusory.

You asserted that our choices are "determined by a set of complicated atomic interactions" because that's what *we are* (a set of complicated atomic interactions), while at the same time you maintain that "this doesn't deprive us of agency." What is agency then? This amounts to, in Jerry Coyne's words, "we can act as if we and others have choices, though we really don't, because what we 'choose' is determined not by our will but by the laws of physics."[9] You said that "we choose what we choose because of who we are; we are who we are because of what we choose." But what exactly do we *choose,* given your metaphysics? As Ed Feser notes, a materialistic world is, by its very definition, one of "purposeless chains of efficient causation," requiring us one of two scenarios: "denying free will outright" or redefining

1. Carroll, "On Determinism," PreposterousUniverse.com.
2. Ibid.
3. Hawking, *The Grand Design*.
4. Baggini and Krauss, "Philosophy v Science", Gaurdian.com.
5. Rosenberg, *The Atheist's Guide to Reality*.
6. Coyne, "Why You Don't Really Have Free Will," USAToday.com.
7. Harris, *Free Will*.
8. Ibid, 18.
9. Coyne, "Sean Carroll on Free Will," WhyEvolutionisTrue.WordPress.com

it so our actions count as "free" (though they really aren't).[10] What is free will if we're simply genetic machines governed solely by the laws of physics and our surroundings? Whether or not we can predict certain actions will be taken is irrelevant. We're just along for the causal ride. We certainly feel we have free will, but it's anything but.

Materialism and Being (Existence and "Well-Being")

To your comment that "we're all part of the causal mesh of the universe." Is the universe its own cause? *Just matter and motion*, without an Unmoved Mover, betrays reason's end, according to Aristotle. In his words, "something else is the cause of the change . . . that from which comes the beginning of the movement" (*Metaphysics, Book 1*). If all contingent things exist in between a state of actuality and potentiality (being), there must be Pure Act (Being Itself). It's not just why anything exists at all (being), but ontological realism (goodness) in nature. Otherwise, how is nature the source of its own being and goodness? Without the ontology of potentiality/actuality (and ends in nature), "well-being" and "goodness" makes no sense objectively. In Aristotle's view, it would be absurd to postulate why matter and motion alone "should be the reason why things manifest goodness and, beauty both in their being and in their coming to be." Aristotle maintained that with Democritus, the question of "whence or how it is to belong to these things" is "lazily neglected" (*Metaphysics, Book 1*).

Thousands of years in advance of the contemporary cosmology of today, Aristotle and Leibniz's great question still remains: "Why is there something rather than nothing?" I've seen materialists go a few ways with this. One I've seen is simply avoiding this question. Another is humility: "*I don't know, but I'm still a materialist.*" A particularly amusing approach (at least to me) is contempt for the big questions such as these, then foolishly proceeding by attacking straw men and fallaciously redefining the word "nothing" in the style of Lawrence Krauss's *A Universe from Nothing*. As philosopher of science David Albert correctly pointed out, quantum vacuums (which Krauss postulates as the source of all existence) are not "nothing."[11] In Aristotelian terms, we would label quantum vacuums "potentiality," so naturally the Aristotelian question follows: where did the quantum vacuums come from? Potentiality requires actuality first. From

10. Feser, *The Last Superstition*, 209.
11. Albert, "On the Origin of Everything," NYTimes.com.

the lens of materialism, the metaphysics of being and "well-being" doesn't add up for me.

Consciousness

In an Aristotelian dance, teleology is inherent in nature, things working towards their ends, given their nature, so on your use of the word "intentionality," suggesting purpose or intention, we agree on much! From bacteria to dolphins to humans, we agree that the more complex the organism (their nature), the more complex their ends. But then our metaphysics clash again! You wrote that "even a bacterium or an amoeba, which I think we agree are fully reducible assemblages of molecules exhibit primitive forms of intentionality." Stop right there, you materialist you! Yes, all life forms pursue certain ends given their nature, but this is not just word play. For an Aristotelian, *there is actual ontological teleology present in nature*. All contingent things exist in between a state of potential and actuality—working towards their "ends." Matter and motion alone are ontologically insufficient. Formal and final causes, potentiality and actuality, complete the picture. Again, our discord is not on accepted scientific knowledge, but on metaphysics.

To stay on the topic of intentionality for a moment, my aim was actually addressing "the problem of intentionality" in philosophy of mind in reducing mind to brain. Here intentionality, is, in philosopher John Searle's words, "the general term for all the various forms by which the mind can be directed at, or be about, or of, objects and states of affairs in the world."[12] The problem with this intentional "aboutness" is reducing subjective, first-person, conscious experience to objective facts. To continue with Searle,

> Conscious states, therefore, have what we might call a "first-person ontology." That is, they exist only from the point of view of some agent or organism or animal or self that has them.... One consequence of the subjectivity of conscious states is that my states of consciousness are accessible to me in a way that they are not accessible to you.... How can that state of my brain—consisting in such things as configurations of neurons and synaptic connections, activated by neurotransmitters—stand for anything?... We

---

12. Searle, *Mind, Language, and Society*, 85.

> are looking for causal mechanisms in the brain. . . . It is internal to the state that it has this intentionality.[13]

My claim that consciousness is irreducible to just matter is not an argument from complexity; it's an argument of principle and ontology. We are the rational animal, a composite of matter and form. Consciousness (and free will) is irreducible (to only matter and motion) *by definition*. Without formal and final causes, there could not be conscious free agency. We agree that the brain is the seat of consciousness and that neuroscience is in its infancy, but knowledge of neuroscience will reveal objective facts and function, not intentional supervenience, formal/final causes (agency), or the irreducible subjective "I" of human experience. To your point:

> If a question seems unanswerable the way it's posed—like "How does the release of chemical signals by neurons give rise to qualia possessing a subjective character of experience?"—that's often a sign that we're not thinking about the problem in the right way. It may be that we don't have the right conceptual framework to approach it in a way that would lead to greater understanding.

My argument is that one million years from now, discoveries in neuroscience will not able to reduce consciousness (formal/final causes, agency, "subjective ontology," intentionality, "qualia-possessing" conscious experience)—by principle. It's not just consciousness, but the entire cosmos. There is more than matter and motion in play with everything in nature. The logic is the same with the "Why is there something rather than nothing?" question. Scientific discoveries (matter and motion) will not be able to explain being from nonbeing. Perhaps, to your point, we're asking the wrong questions. Perhaps we don't have the cognitive capacity to even grasp the matter, perhaps we never will. Perhaps we need to discover some other fundamental truths about neuroscience or the universe in general. I think we are asking the right questions, we always have, and that the answers to the big questions lie beyond matter and motion.

* * *

I'd love to turn the page to the application of our worldviews on how to move towards the just city in a pluralistic society. We've had some fantastic back and forth at our debates on the separation of church and state,

---

13. Ibid., 42–43, 89–90, 96–97.

healthcare, abortion, etc. Before jumping in, I'd love your thoughts on President Obama's sentiments:

> Democracy demands that the religiously motivated translate their concerns into universal, rather than religion-specific, values. It requires that their proposals be subject to argument, and amenable to reason. I may be opposed to abortion for religious reasons, but if I seek to pass a law banning the practice, I cannot simply point to the teachings of my church or [invoke] God's will. I have to explain why abortion violates some principle that is accessible to people of all faiths, including those with no faith at all.[14]

I think we agree on universal principles guiding legislation. Politically, I think we're both unimpressed with conservative tribalism, though I must admit I'm equally unimpressed by liberal tribalism. As an independent, I'm unimpressed with tribalism in general. What is "justice," in a universal sense, and how do we move towards such a republic?

---

14. Obama, "Call to Renewal, Keynote Address."

META

I must intreat you to inquire what the knowledge is, that you learn from your spiritual teachers. "The knowledge by faith," they will answer for you. "And faith," they will add, "is the knowledge of things unseen."

Can there be any such knowledge? I put it to your reason. Knowledge we have shown to be ascertained facts. Things unseen! Can human understanding know anything about them? More I will ask: could it be of any utility were even such knowledge possible? And do ye hire teachers to teach you non-existent knowledge, impossible knowledge, and knowledge which, even under the supposition of its possibility, could serve no conceivable purpose?[15]

—FRANCES WRIGHT

Andrew,

Well, so far this little conversation of ours has focused more on the God part than on government. I'm glad to get into the other side of things, but first I want to return to a few points from the last installment that will be relevant to our new topic.

Axioms, Falsifiability, and Word Games

Last time, I asked you how you can be certain that God is good and not evil, given that you don't claim to understand his goals or motivations. You said:

> If you recall from our back and forth on morality, "good," in an Aristotelian-Thomistic view, is simply "well-being." In this conception, being and goodness are inseparable concepts. Because there is being and goodness in nature, there is a Source (Being and Goodness). Thus, asking "What if Pure Act (Infinite Being and Infinite Goodness) is actually bad?" is nonsensical. The necessary truths of God's nature are similar to other necessary truths such as the nature of a triangle. Trying to separate goodness from God, in the classical conception, is like trying to ask "what if 2+2=5?"

You can say that a triangle axiomatically has three sides or that two plus two axiomatically equals four, and I won't argue. But goodness is

15. Wright, *Course of Popular Lectures*, 72.

A/theological and Metaphysical Puzzles, Part III

nothing like this. It's neither a logical axiom nor a mathematical necessity, but a complex and contingent judgment derived from reasoned evaluation of a person's actions. In other words, it is—and must be—*a posteriori* rather than *a priori*.

From my perspective, you've addressed one paradox by introducing a different one. If God isn't a contingent being existing in a state between potentiality and actuality, then it's not clear how God can *act* at all. To act, to decide, to make choices: all these things require the ability to select among potentials and turn one into actuality. If there were a God whose nature was "infinitely different" than our own, how would we even begin to talk about such a being? By definition, it would be utterly impossible for us to explain, understand, or describe. Yet millions of religious people feel very confident proclaiming their beliefs about God's will as absolute fact. It's only when atheists point out the logical problems with these ideas that they recede into vagueness and ambiguity.

This is the larger problem I have with most theologies: however lofty they sound, they turn out to be just mystery piled upon mystery. Saying that God is pure actuality, or that teleology is an intrinsic quality of the universe, or that goodness exists in ontological reality—these are all just words. They don't *explain* anything. They don't give us insight, don't advance our understanding, don't give us the ability to predict what will or won't happen. However grand an intellectual edifice it may be, it's sterile in an explanatory sense.

A good scientific hypothesis tells us what further questions we should ask. It predicts surprising, counterintuitive consequences that can be verified by observation. It unites diverse phenomena under a single theoretical umbrella. This Aristotelian theology, as far as I can tell, doesn't do any of those things. Logicians and theologians can slap together whatever axioms they choose, but if they don't have testable claims to tie their ideas to reality, all it amounts to is playing games with words.

Freedoms Worth Wanting

You raised some critiques regarding my view of free will, which I'd like to address here:

> What is free will if we're simply genetic machines governed solely by the laws of physics and our surroundings? Whether or not we can predict certain actions will be taken is irrelevant. We're just

along for the causal ride. We certainly feel we have free will, but it's anything but.

If you define free will as the ability to defy the laws of physics—to make a choice which stands outside the causal chain that governs everything else in the universe—then as a materialist, I have to agree that we don't have that kind of free will. We make choices in accordance with our nature. But that's true of everything and everyone, even (in your view) God, so I don't see what that deprives us of.

I'm happy to accept that the choices I make are determined by a vast and complex network of causes acting on me (some of which, as I said earlier, are my own past choices). I'm happy to accept this, because it leaves room for moral teaching and learning, for improving with experience, for recognizing bad habits and poor patterns of behavior and breaking out of them. All of these are specifically *causal* abilities, things that are only possible if our choices are made for reasons.

If free will is truly causeless, determined by nothing, then it must be like a lightning strike: something that randomly imposes itself on me, something that's unrelated to who I am or what I desire. Who would want that kind of free will? What makes those decisions *mine*, if they're unconnected to the state of my brain, the habits of past experience, or my wishes at any given moment?

I can't escape the conclusion that supernatural indeterminism, even if it were true, wouldn't give us any kind of free will "worth wanting," as Daniel Dennett puts it.[16] If anything, true indeterminism would make us *less* free by thwarting our efforts to control our behavior and change it for the better. It's our ability to understand the workings of our material brains that makes that kind of self-improvement possible.

Multiplying Entities beyond Necessity

You said that materialism has no clear answer to the question, "Why is there something rather than nothing?" For all that it's made up of words put together in a syntactically valid way, I have my doubts as to whether this is a meaningful question. What could possibly count as an answer? Any causal factor that I might invoke to explain the universe's existence would itself be a part of that pre-existing "something" that has to be explained.

---

16. Dennett, *Elbow Room*, 1.

However, I emphasize that theism has no superior solution to this problem. Just the same way, an atheist can ask "Why is there a god rather than no god?" No matter what answer anyone might give to that question, an atheist can apply it in a parallel way. If you follow Aristotle in saying that god is "pure being" and doesn't need an external cause, then a materialist like me could take the parallel tack of asserting that the universe as a whole is "pure being" and requires no explanation outside itself.

In some ways, that explanation could even be *better*, in the Occam's razor sense of philosophical simplicity. There's no reason why the substrate of existence has to be conscious, purposeful, aware of our existence, concerned for our well-being, benevolent, loving, or any of the other humanlike qualities traditionally ascribed to God. These are all complicated, contingent traits that I see no reason to impose on nature. Doing so multiplies entities beyond necessity, which is just what Occam's razor warns us against.

This is what I mean when I say that most theology is unfalsifiable. Is there any way to verify the proposition that "pure being" is also the source of ontological goodness? Is this something that can be put to the test, something that can prove its superiority to different alternatives, or is it something you just have to believe? Does it even express a meaningful proposition about reality?

By contrast, it's clear what my atheistic materialism means. Moral goodness, intentionality, consciousness itself—all these are qualities that *we* create. We bring them into being by virtue of our existence. That makes us, intelligent beings, genuinely special and extraordinary. Without us, the universe would just be "rocks moving in curves," as Terry Pratchett said.[17]

That's also why it's so important for all of us to exercise independent judgment, rather than suspending one's moral faculties and relying solely on religious text and doctrine for morality. If you start down this road, you're treading a very slippery slope indeed. If you start with the belief that God is necessarily good and should be obeyed and trusted no matter what, you'll shortly arrive at the corollary that people who speak for God are partaking of God's necessarily good nature, and should also be obeyed and trusted, even when their actions run contrary to what we would otherwise understand as morality. And anyone who's familiar with history knows what kind of horrors that way of thinking will have you defending.

---

17. Pratchett, *Hogfather*, 289.

Slavery, which is condoned and approved in the Bible, is just one example of many I could give. The slaveholders of the American antebellum endlessly quoted the Bible as proof that God, who is "necessarily good," was supporting them and approved of their actions. The medieval Catholic Church also got in on the act with the papal bull *Dum diversas*, which gave Christian kings the right to enslave nonbelievers defeated in battle. How can you persuade someone otherwise when they start with premises like these?

The quote you gave from Barack Obama, which I like very much, is a clear illustration of this point. If you organize society such that one sect's interpretation of God's will is allowed to reign supreme, morality becomes arbitrary. Debate and persuasion become impossible, and force is the only resort for dealing with dissent. But if society is based on secular reasoning—if you can't use "God is necessarily good and he told me he wants us to do X" as the basis for law-making, but must make your arguments on the basis of evidence that others can examine—then we human beings can reason together and reach a democratic consensus on how to proceed.

And I'll let that be my segue, as I turn to the topic of justice in society. To your question, "What is 'justice', in a universal sense, and how do we move towards such a republic?"—I think a useful starting point for this question is John Rawls's classic thought experiment. Imagine designing a society—its laws and its institutions—from behind a veil of ignorance. When you've completed your blueprint, you'll be born into the society you designed, but without knowing in advance who you'll be or where you'll end up. If you might be the poorest, most disadvantaged member of your society, then it pays to make sure that even the poorest and most disadvantaged member of your society isn't treated too badly. A civilization that embodies this principle, I think, is one that upholds what we call justice.

Obviously, there's no veil of ignorance in the real world, except in this sense: None of us can choose the time or place of our birth. Some of us are born into privilege, others into poverty. Now, if a society is truly based on merit, then accidents of birth won't matter, because we'll each rise or fall according to our inherent talents, skills, and determination. Everyone will wind up in the place they earned for themselves by their own effort, which is what we can call justice.

But I'd argue that our society is far from this ideal. The time, place, and circumstances of your birth matter a great deal, both in tangible aspects like the quality of your education or your ability to get healthcare, as well

A/theological and Metaphysical Puzzles, Part III

as less concrete factors, like whether you happen to be born into a religion that's socially dominant and that controls the levers of power and influence in your society.

I believe this state of affairs needs to change. Even if we never reach the ideal of perfect justice and fairness, we can approach it as closely as possible. And to do that, we'll use the tool you described, democratic persuasion based on secular reasoning. By showing people the extent of injustice in our society, awakening their conscience to evils they've overlooked, we can persuade them to support the eradication of those evils through legal change and cultural pressure.

And I think that religion is and will always be an obstacle to this process, for the reasons I've laid out: because religious morality isn't based on evidence, it encourages people to dig in their heels against democratic persuasion, and to treat evils tolerated in their culture as the immutable will of God, who only commands what is good even if we can't see how that's so.

How does this position match up with yours? What do you think we can do to persuade people who use religion to justify evil?

ROUND 11

From Metaphysics to Natural Rights and Abortion, Part I

We hold these truths to be self-evident, that all men are created equal, that they are endowed by their Creator with certain unalienable Rights, that among these are Life, Liberty and the pursuit of Happiness.

—US DECLARATION OF INDEPENDENCE

Adam,

Throughout the course of our exchange, I continue to be reminded by the fact that philosophical presuppositions are often at the root of discord on practical and political positions. Rather than overlook these important issues and proceed with haste and hostility, I've thoroughly enjoyed the deep dive into the metaphysical baggage.

Politically, we're both aligned with the spirit of the Obama quote. We agree that an equal and free society, legislating from universal principles, is the only way true democracy can proceed—perhaps more eloquently stated above by our founding fathers. If we're aiming to legislate from universal principles, we should reason from universal principles. This, of course, is built off the assumption that there is such a thing as objective goodness that we have free will to reason towards.

In keeping with the theme of political views and underlying philosophical presuppositions, I'll shape my reply by going back into the metaphysical drawer, then put forward the topic of abortion which I find is frequently laced with hostility, haste, and ambiguity.

Back to Metaphysics

As a natural rights theorist, I maintain that every person has intrinsic rights of equal value and there is an objective good for us to seek and reach, given our nature. This is built off my hylomorphic and teleological view of nature. My theism, as I've noted previously, comes in at the end of the picture as reason's end of being and goodness. For you, reason's end is materialism. You mentioned Occam's razor and how materialism is more philosophically simple and clear and that theism degrades into obscurity and word games. As you might expect, I'm at the opposite end of the spectrum. To me there is no better word play than materialists attempting to ground being, moral ontology, and free will.

On being—"Why is there something rather than nothing?"—you find this to be a meaningless question. To many, especially those metaphysically inclined, this is *the* question. You either dismiss it or assert "that the universe as a whole is 'pure being' and requires no explanation outside itself." But how is the universe itself metaphysically Necessary—the cause of its own existence? The principle of causation is the basis of reason, science, and common sense. Everything in the universe is contingent and operates under causal principles, but suddenly the universe as a whole is "Being Itself"? To me this is textbook infinite regress and obscurantism.

I get materialism. I also get Occam's razor. What I don't get is combining them on being, goodness, and free will. If I were a materialist, I'd argue by Occam's razor that there is no morality or free will (as the thinkers I cited last round maintain). Moral goodness, you penned, "we create" which "makes us, intelligent beings, genuinely special and extraordinary," and a materialist free will is one that "leaves room for moral teaching and learning, for improving with experience, for recognizing bad habits and poor patterns of behavior and breaking out of them." This is poetic, but metaphysically bankrupt. If we create morality, what's objective? What's special and extraordinary about selfish genes acting in a way in which there is no other possibility? Behavior, as Alex Rosenberg maintains, would simply be "determined," like "dominos" toppling in a row, "beyond our control . . . not something for which we can be blamed, or praised for that matter."[1]

---

1. Rosenberg, *Philosophy of Science*, 8.

Where is there room for breaking out of bad habits if we're material robots helplessly along for the ride? Perhaps we break out of bad habits, perhaps we don't—either way, there is no actual freedom.

With hylomorphism, I gave a conception of free will, consciousness, and moral objectivity that is neither spooky nor involves violating the laws of physics—though it does involve formal and final causes in nature that are precluded in the materialist's toolbox. That said, allow me to clarify some things on "goodness." To your comment:

> You can say that a triangle axiomatically has three sides or that two plus two axiomatically equals four, and I won't argue. But goodness is nothing like this. It's neither a logical axiom nor a mathematical necessity, but a complex and contingent judgment derived from reasoned evaluation of a person's actions. In other words, it is—and must be—*a posteriori* rather than *a priori*.

Let's be careful to not conflate ontology and metaethics with epistemology and practical ethics. I did not say goodness is like mathematics, fixed truths which I can access infallibly from the armchair, nor did I say I understand what the good is in every possible case. I maintained that there is such thing as objective goodness ontologically, that nature is an irreducible composite of matter and form, and that all contingent things exist in between a state of potentiality and actuality. Again, good is just "well-being," something pursuing its end to a certain degree, given its nature. From my experience of particulars, I reason *a posteriori* towards universals (scientific truths, mathematical truths, moral truths, etc.).

God's existence is no different. Because anything exists at all, because there is objective goodness, because all contingent things exist in between a state of potentiality and actuality, I reason towards God as Pure Act, the Unmoved Mover, and Necessity of which all contingent things depend. Goodness itself is not a necessary truth, but God as Pure Act (Being and Goodness Itself) is a necessary truth in the Aristotelian-Thomistic conception (goodness being inseparable from God's nature). This is simply my ontological accounting of goodness.

To your question, "is this something that can be put to the test, something that can prove its superiority to different alternatives"—it is falsifiable? Of course it is—*rationally and metaphysically*. Remember the case for theism or materialism is a philosophical one. Demanding God as a scientific hypothesis is to slip into scientism, which is extremely problematic and question-begging. Rationally, I maintain that the universe has a transcendent Cause—otherwise it's its own cause. Is it meaningful? Of course it is—*the universe has a meaning*—otherwise we just "make up" meaning. This is why I maintain that in a sound metaphysics of being, theism is reason's end. Without God, Pure Act, Being and Goodness Itself, being and objective goodness is impossible. If there is a superior rational and metaphysically coherent alternative to existence, morality, free will, and some of the other big questions we've discussed, let's hear it! In my view, it certainly isn't materialism.

You contended that God being infinite (Necessary, Pure Act, Being Itself), precludes us (contingent beings) from being able to have any such knowledge of Him. True, we can only have finite knowledge (as we're finite creatures) of God, but it does not follow that any knowledge of God is impossible. We can experience God through our finite metaphysical lenses. I've given extensive arguments for the rational/metaphysical arguments for God's existence as well as the "experience of God."

I would agree with you on the value of *a posteriori* moral reasoning, but take issue with "*a posteriori* rather than *a priori*." Ethics can't be just *a posteriori*. Reasoned evaluation to what measure? What is the nature of humanity? What does "well-being" mean? We all have first principles. As Peter Singer correctly notes, all ethical theories "must rest on a fundamental intuition about what is good."[2] If you recall, you defended your definition of "goodness" from first principles:

> When it comes to atheistic moral skeptics, as I said, I'm aware that I can't convince someone who disagrees with me on first principles. The only answer I can give them is the same answer anyone can ever give to any kind of philosophical skeptic: namely, a practical answer ("I refute it thus!").

From Metaphysics to Politics

Let's turn the page to practical ethics and politics. Though we differ on theism and materialism on reason's end, we agree on the centrality of reason in democracy. As I've maintained from go, reason is the bedrock of my faith, so in dismissing any theists that wish to divorce their faith from reason, we stand together.

---

2. Singer, "Ethics and Intuitions," 349.

META

We also agree that because our reasoning is limited and fallible, we *absolutely* need empirical validation. If you recall from our morality discussion, we agreed that moral armchair reasoning blind to consequence or universal principles is simple fanaticism. Many theistic and atheistic fanatic regimes that preached "duty" were simply crimes against humanity.

I think Rawls's thought experiment is fantastic because it encourages universal empathy. Universal empathy speaks to the Golden Rule, which as a Christian, I feel is a core philosophy. On the fanatics who justified slavery in the name of God, I would say Google "abolitionism" or "William Wilberforce" to learn about Christians who gave their lives to fight against such fanaticism. To your point:

> And I think that religion is and will always be an obstacle to this process, for the reasons I've laid out: because religious morality isn't based on evidence, it encourages people to dig in their heels against democratic persuasion, and to treat evils tolerated in their culture as the immutable will of God, who only commands what is good even if we can't see how that's so. How does this position match up with yours? What do you think we can do to persuade people who use religion to justify evil?

I think we agree on fanaticism, but we may disagree on religion's net negative contribution to humanity, so I'll trade a few of your words with mine (in italics) to illustrate: "And I think that *fanaticism* is and will always be an obstacle to this process . . . because *fanaticism* isn't based on evidence, it encourages people to dig in their heels . . . and to treat evils tolerated in their culture as the immutable will of *Hitler*."

On "democratic persuasion," I don't think either of us wants to tally up fanatic state atheism vs. fantastic state theism for crimes against humanity. Fanaticism itself has a nasty record, regardless of the state irreligion/religion. Any system of morality blind to evidence is dangerous. Any worldview, including atheism, infused with a few doses of fanatical tribalism and the right spark, can lead to terror. Thus, I think a better question would be: "*How can we persuade fanatics who use any worldview to justify evil?*" For that my answer would be transcendence. In the example and words of Martin Luther King Jr.:

> Returning hate for hate multiplies hate, adding deeper darkness to a night already devoid of stars. Darkness cannot drive out

darkness; only light can do that. Hate cannot drive out hate; only love can do that.[3]

You fight hatred with love, ignorance with education/awareness, inertia with persistence. In the Christian narrative, one of my favorite verses comes to mind: "The light shines in the darkness, and the darkness has not overcome it" (John 1:5). Again, we may not agree on the metaphysical accounting, but we do agree on key universals (life, liberty, happiness, equality). Legislation on universal principles is a natural extension! As tyranny is the enemy of freedom, we don't just persuade against it. We march against it. We legislate against it. Democracy demands nothing less.

We've exchanged quite a bit on metaphysics, morality, and legislating on universal principles—shall we extend this into abortion? I'd like to get past the typical tribalistic discussion and learn more about your specific views, as we're both truth seekers who espouse moral realism. If we were moral skeptics/nihilists/relativists, it would be a pretty quick discussion. Let's not jump out of the gates on "right to life" or "right to choose"—let's hold off on the legislative aspect for a moment. Philosophically, what are your thoughts on abortion? At what point (if any) during pregnancy does it become immoral to have an abortion? If you and your wife were pregnant but it was not the ideal time to have a child, would you proceed, no-brainer, to an abortion?

---

3. King, Jr., *Strength to Love*, 53.

META

Prayer seems to me a cry of weakness, and an attempt to avoid, by trickery, the rules of the game as laid down. I do not choose to admit weakness. I accept the challenge of responsibility. Life, as it is, does not frighten me, since I have made my peace with the universe as I find it, and bow to its laws.... It seems to me that organized creeds are collections of words around a wish. I feel no need for such.... The springing of the yellow line of morning out of the misty deep of dawn, is glory enough for me. I know that nothing is destructible; things merely change forms. When the consciousness we know as life ceases, I know that I shall still be part and parcel of the world. I was a part before the sun rolled into shape and burst forth in the glory of change. I was, when the earth was hurled out from its fiery rim. I shall return with the earth to Father Sun, and still exist in substance when the sun has lost its fire, and disintegrated into infinity to perhaps become a part of the whirling rubble of space. Why fear? The stuff of my being is matter, ever changing, ever moving, but never lost; so what need of denominations and creeds to deny myself the comfort of all my fellow men?[4]

—ZORA NEALE HURSTON

Andrew,

I'm ready to move on to comparing our views on government, but first I'd like to request clarification on one small point:

> Goodness itself is not a necessary truth, but God as Pure Act (Being and Goodness Itself) is a necessary truth in the Aristotelian-Thomistic conception, (goodness being inseparable from God's nature).

I've read this over, but I'm afraid I'm still confused. Maybe this question will clarify the difference between us: In your view, is God a moral epiphenomenon? When you or I are faced with an ethical dilemma, I assume we'd handle it in generally the same way: decide which moral principles are relevant, sum up the balance of competing interests, and make the choice that we believe will accomplish the most good. At what point does God enter into this process? Is God's will a trump card that overrules other factors? Does God provide some kind of communication to "double-check"

---

4. Hurston, *Dust Tracks on a Road*, 226.

the final decision before you act on it? If not, I'm just not seeing how your moral philosophy differs from that of an atheist like me.

Of course, now that we're turning to more specific political questions, maybe that will be an opportunity to illuminate the differences between us. If you'd like to show me how this works in some concrete examples, I'd be interested to hear it. To your point:

> Any system of morality blind to evidence is dangerous. Any worldview, including atheism, infused with a few doses of fanatical tribalism and the right spark, can lead to terror.

I couldn't agree more! As I said at an earlier stage of our conversation, morality must always be empirical if it's to avoid disastrous error. I've often argued that the core flaw of the communist regimes was that they were *so* convinced they possessed absolute truth, *so* certain that history had a preordained end and they were its servants, that they believed they were justified in committing whatever cruelty was necessary to bring about the promised ultimate utopia.

In this respect, communism bears a striking similarity to fundamentalist religion. Both have a set of inflexible and all-encompassing dogmas, handed down from the founders, that have to be followed to the letter and can never be allowed to fail. With religion, it's obedience to the will of God, as taught and interpreted by religious authorities; with communism, it's devotion to the all-powerful state and the wisdom of the supreme leader.

If following those rules produces bad results, it's not because the rules themselves are bad, but only because the people aren't strong enough or devoted enough to follow them properly. There's no allowance for questioning, no possibility for debate. And because the authorities possess a complete and infallible vision of the good, anyone who dissents from that vision must be evil, and should be silenced so as not to lead others astray.

But for all the similarities, there's one important difference between the two. Namely, since it was a materialist ideology, communism could only make promises about what would happen in *this* world. This means that even the most fanatical communist regimes eventually had to deliver the goods. They could churn out propaganda, suppress free speech and media, and imprison dissidents, but they couldn't prevent people from seeing for themselves how badly things were going. They couldn't keep everyone from noticing that communism didn't deliver the glorious utopia it promised. I'm certain that this is a major reason why communist states have collapsed or shifted to other forms of government all over the world.

META

When you import the supernatural into your moral system, you lose even that minimal reality check. You can persuade people to labor all their life, in poverty and deprivation, by promising them vast rewards in a heavenly afterlife whose existence can't be verified. You can cow them into obedience by threatening them with a hellish afterlife of torture if they disobey. Or you can simply decree that the rules are not to be questioned, even if they seem cruel or unreasonable, because God's ways are infinitely higher than ours and we have no right to pass judgment on the results.

To me, that's the appeal of atheism, humanism, and skepticism: it denies the authority of dogmas both earthly and heavenly. When a power-hungry politician promises that absolute obedience to his commands will lead to glory and prosperity, we skeptics can say, "Prove it." When a tyrannical regime tries to shut down all dissent, we humanists can observe that such a grave violation of human rights inevitably leads to further evils. And when an anointed leader claims to have access to a higher morality than the rest of us, we atheists can argue that there's only one world, and no one has knowledge of something that exists outside it.

You asked:

> Philosophically, what are your thoughts on abortion? At what point (if any) during pregnancy does it become immoral to have an abortion?

Ah, now we're getting to the interesting stuff! The hardest moral dilemmas are the ones that involve a genuine clash of interests, and though I personally consider myself pro-choice, this isn't a case where all the arguments point the same way.

I think there are some ground rules everyone would agree on. Any conscious, thinking, feeling being has a right not to be arbitrarily killed. In addition, we recognize that there are circumstances under which there exists a duty of care. Parents certainly don't have the right to abandon or neglect children who are too young to fend for themselves.

On the other hand, people also have a right to exercise control and autonomy over their own bodies. Indeed, that's the most basic and fundamental right of all: the right of self-ownership.

I can't force you to donate a kidney to me, even if you're the only compatible donor in the world and I'll die without a transplant. Even if you agree to donate the kidney and later change your mind, no ethical surgeon would tell you that it's too late to back out and try to operate on you against your will. The idea of organ harvesting from an unwilling donor is an evil that shocks the conscience, as it should be. I just don't see how it changes this calculus if the organ is a uterus, rather than a kidney or a lung.

In my view, if it were purely a matter of these two rights colliding, the bodily autonomy principle would win out. I have the right to live, if I'm capable of doing so without extraordinary means, but I don't have the right to parasitize the body of an unwilling other for sustenance. (And "parasitize" is absolutely the right word—in pregnancy, there's a very real conflict between the fetus and the mother for resources. It's widely believed that the life-threatening condition of preeclampsia arises when the fetus grows too rapidly and tries to siphon off a greater share of blood flow and nutrients than the mother's body can safely provide.)[5]

But what makes the decision easier is that, for most of the span of a pregnancy, the fetus's brain hasn't developed to the point where conscious thought or feeling is possible. Insofar as that's the case, there aren't two separate people whose interests may collide; there's only one person, the mother. A fetus without a fully developed brain is merely a potential person, and isn't the sort of entity in which the rights of personhood can vest.

You asked if my wife and I were pregnant but it was not the ideal time, would I "proceed, 'no-brainer,' to an abortion?" Yes! I would never counsel anyone to go through with a pregnancy if they weren't confident that they were ready—physically, financially, and emotionally—to assume the enormous responsibility of parenthood. The consequences are far too great to be thrust upon someone who isn't prepared for them. It's not fair to force anyone to give up their own hopes and aspirations for life to care for a child they didn't want to have, and it's not fair to that child to be brought into the world by parents who'll resent its existence or who don't have the means to protect and care for it.

I would, of course, acknowledge that adoption should also be available as an option, for those who choose it. Even so, it's a fact that pregnancy often entails hardship, suffering, and very real risks to the woman's health and even her life. The idea of forcing someone to bear that burden against their will is horrifying, probably the most intimate and outrageous violation of personal liberty imaginable. A wanted pregnancy is a beautiful thing, a choice that bespeaks hope for the future and the desire to bring a unique and precious new life into the world, and deserves society's respect and protection. But coerced pregnancy and childbirth is abhorrent in equal measure.

5. Espinoza and Espinoza, "Pre-Eclampsia," 367–70.

ROUND 12

From Metaphysics to Natural Rights and Abortion, Part II

I do, as a humanist, believe that the concept "unborn child" is a real one and I think the concept is underlined by all the recent findings of embryology about the early viability of a well-conceived human baby, one that isn't going to be critically deformed, or even some that are, will be able to survive outside the womb earlier and earlier, and I see that date only being pushed back and I feel the responsibility to consider the occupant of the womb as a candidate member of society in the future, and thus to say that it cannot be only the responsibility of the woman to decide upon it, that it's a social question and an ethical and a moral one. And I say this as someone who has no supernatural belief.[1]

—CHRISTOPHER HITCHENS

Adam,

I think you put forward some great points for discussion. First, I'll address the metaphysics, then move onto the politics with abortion.

Metaphysics

In the Aristotelian-Thomistic view, God is the furthest thing from a moral epiphenomenon. God is the source of existence and goodness, Being and

---

1. Hitchens, Debate with Turek, "Does God Exist?"

Goodness Itself, the Final Cause, and Necessity of which all contingent things depend. As all contingent things exist in between a state of potentiality and actuality, well-being (morality/goodness) is simply things working well towards certain ends, given their nature.

To your point on practicality, I agree we approach many moral decisions in a similar way. Aristotelian metaphysics views humans as the rational and social animal, so morality is simply acting to our potential as rational and social beings. In the vein of practical ethics, your and Sam Harris's views are like mine. Empiricism is crucial in guiding us to make the just and good decision for human well-being.

Ours is a not a disagreement of practical ethics, but metaphysics and metaethics, in defining what "good," "happiness," and "well-being" mean in an objective sense. Aristotle's morality is built on his teleological and hylomorphic view of nature, which materialism rejects. Rejecting God, in my view, amounts to rejecting the metaphysical source of being and goodness—so "well-being," "goodness," and "happiness" are ultimately subjective.

On dogmatism, we agree on much, but I take issue with the assertion that "when you import the supernatural into your moral system, you lose even that minimal reality check" and that "you can persuade people to labor all their life, in poverty and deprivation, by promising them vast rewards in an afterlife whose existence can't be verified."

I disagree on three key points. First, people with no minimal reality check are dogmatic by definition, regardless of their religious beliefs. Secondly, though it's true that materialist ideologies themselves are obviously devoid of any supernatural elements, *atheism is not secular humanism*. Your "prove it" challenge goes both ways. Many atheists and skeptics find secular humanism quite religious and claim the logical consequence of materialism is moral non-realism/nihilism/relativism. To that point, many crimes against humanity have been performed, in the minds of their perpetrators, *in the name of God* and *because there is no God*. Any worldview that invites in dogmatic fanaticism loses a minimal reality check. Thirdly, a Christian who "persuades people to labor all their life in poverty and deprivation by promising them vast rewards in an afterlife" ceases *to be a Christian in those actions,* just as a Nazi atheist *ceases to be a humanist* when he leads someone into a gas chamber. Sincere Christians draw immense virtue from their supernatural beliefs that are directly imported into their love and service of others, just as several atheists draw virtue from the spirit of their secular humanism.

META

The arguments for/against God's existence aren't going anywhere, so I would argue that "theism" and "atheism" should only be the beginning of one's philosophy—universal empathy hopefully a next step for both camps. We can argue about metaphysics and metaethics over a cup of coffee as friends. On practical ethics, we agree on much and this can be a launch pad for us to work together to change the world. Universal crimes against humanity—genocide, slavery, and human trafficking, for example—should be fought universally. I would also tack on ir/religious persecution—another area of agreement. If we both stand together and act towards universal empathy (legislation, social justice, etc.), we'll change the world.

Abortion

As I mentioned earlier, I believe abortion is a highly polarizing topic given its philosophical underpinnings. I think the challenge (both in meaningful discussion and in legislation) is, again, arguing from universals (not emotions, presuppositions, or tradition), so I'll make that my aim for this discussion. On your sentiments:

> Any conscious, thinking, feeling being has a right to continued existence and to not be arbitrarily killed. . . . Parents certainly don't have the right to abandon or neglect their children who are too young to fend for themselves. . . . People also have a right to exercise control and autonomy over their own bodies. . . . I don't have the right to parasitize the body of an unwilling other for sustenance.

Agreed! But the slope gets very slippery extending these arguments into the nuances of abortion. On the *parasite argument*, you "parasiting" off an innocent person against their consent would be immoral, but allow me to expand via two scenarios: A ("Evil Adam") and B ("Fetus Adam"). Evil Adam is a mad scientist with a fatal blood disease. The only way he can survive is if he can be implanted into the lungs of another human being and parasite off their lung tissue. To his luck, he's created a way to miniaturize himself in a pod and enter human beings through their nostrils. He's successfully implanted himself into his first victim and is en route to their lungs. Fetus Adam was conceived by the consensual act of his parents. My point: A is not B.

If I found out "Evil Adam" was in me, I would have every right to defend myself. But "Fetus Adam" was conceived by two consenting adults, knowing full well that a developing human being will/may be the consequence. Adam's parents decide they do not want the baby so they decide on abortion. In killing "Evil Adam" vs. "Fetus Adam," is there a moral difference?

Before we get into rights, pain, or consciousness, I wanted to first get your thoughts on atheist philosopher Don Marquis's view that abortion is immoral *prima facie* (from a purely humanistic view)—regardless of "rights" or "brain activity"—it's wrong. His "deprivation argument" claims that it's wrong to kill any human being because it deprives them of a valuable future (memories, life, experience, etc.), fetuses also have a valuable future, so killing a fetus is wrong.[2] Can one maintain that this living and developing fetus also has rights and it is *prima facie* wrong to kill it?

In his book, *Moral Tribes*, moral philosopher Joshua Greene (also an atheist) puts out a pro-choice challenge: "to be a coherent pro-choicer, one must explain why early-term abortions are morally acceptable but late-term abortions are not."[3] Let's assume at time X in the term, thought and feeling is possible. Would you agree that "late-term" (past that point) and partial-birth abortions are immoral? What if a mother at that point changed her mind and wanted to abort? Should it be illegal to drive forceps into the brain of "the parasite" during delivery? If we go with "rights," if "the parasite" is still "in the mother"—we're golden, right? If not, is it rights, pain, or consciousness? What is the exact balance where it's morally permissible? In the case of partial-birth abortion, one could easily argue that a woman's rights are violated if she's forced to deliver.

Pain seems like a self-evident dividing line at first blush, but things also get tricky here. If you go with the *pain argument,* you run immediately into the evidence of brain waves at seven weeks—the pain argument could start right there. The second problem, as relates to the first, is that pain is not consciousness (rationality, self-awareness, etc.).[4] Philosopher Marry Anne Warren tries to address these ambiguities in her criteria for "personhood" to provide a coherent argument in support of abortion. The problem is that her argument extends to infanticide. In her words,

---

2. Marquis, "Why Abortion is Immoral," 183–202.
3. Greene, *Moral Tribes,* 310.
4. Gordon, *Internet Encyclopedia of Philosophy,* s.v. "Abortion."

META

> It remains true that according to my argument neither abortion nor the killing of neonates is properly considered a form of murder.[5]

"Consciousness" is another tough one. What is the difference in "consciousness" between an eight-month fetus that is about to die via late-term abortion, a nine-month fetus that is about to die via partial-birth abortion, and a newly delivered baby that is about to be murdered? To Peter Singer's point, there is not "a morally significant line of demarcation between an embryo and a newborn baby." He continues:

> The standard liberal position needs to be able to point to some such line, because liberals usually hold that it is permissible to kill an embryo or fetus but not a baby.... Now we have to face the fact that these arguments apply to the newborn baby as much as to the fetus. A week-old baby is not a rational and self-aware being.... If, for the reasons I have given, the fetus does not have the same claim to life as a person, it appears that the newborn baby does not either. Thus, although my position on the status of fetal life may be acceptable to many, the implications of this position for the status of newborn life are at odds with the virtually unchallenged assumption that the life of a newborn baby is as sacrosanct as that of an adult.[6]

If the cut-off is "conscious/thinking" and this means rational, self-reflecting beings, why does a newborn get special status if they don't qualify as such? The issue for me here is arbitrariness. This should be a logical argument, not an emotional one. To conclude with some closing thoughts from Greene:

> In sum, to construct a coherent justification for the pro-choice position on abortion is actually very hard.... In our popular moral discourse, it's perfectly accessible to say, "I believe in a woman's right to choose," without further explanation. But without further explanation, appealing to this "right" is just a bluff, a bald assertion to the effect that, somewhere out there, there is a coherent, pro-choice theory of reproductive rights.[7]

Let's say I were a secular humanist but wanted very hard to grab onto a coherent and consistent pro-choice theory. Could you address these objections for me?

5. Warren, "On the Moral and Legal Status of Abortion."
6. Singer, *Practical Ethics*, 151.
7. Greene, *Moral Tribes*, 312–13.

From Metaphysics to Natural Rights and Abortion, Part II

The Protestant right and the Catholic hierarchy say that abortion is murder because they regard even a day-old collection of cells as a human being—a person capable of being murdered. Most Jews, mainstream Protestants, liberal Catholics, and atheists do not regard abortion as murder because they do not believe that the embryo or fetus—at least not before it can survive outside the mother's body—is a person. The battle over abortion is a quarrel not between relativists who favor murder and absolutists who oppose it but between competing definitions of whether a fetus is a person to whom the term murder can even be applied.[8]

—SUSAN JACOBY, *FREETHINKERS*

Andrew,

It seems to me that you see God not as a divine being who communicates directly with people to give us commands, but rather as an abstract principle of goodness whose "will" can only be discerned by balancing the needs and desires of human beings. This sounds closer to what I would call deism than to conventional orthodox Christianity. Or am I missing something? Do you believe that God gives people commands through special revelation?

The reason I ask is that the Bible doesn't give much support to this distant and impersonal deity of the philosophers. It depicts God as a being with wishes, desires, and preferences who acts in history. An abstract principle of ultimate goodness or a transcendent Final Cause couldn't give stone tablets to Moses on a mountaintop, or be incarnated in the body of Jesus and rise from the dead post-crucifixion. If you treat these stories as metaphors, fair enough, but if they're *all* metaphors, then you may be closer to my viewpoint than I had guessed!

We also spoke about the reality check inherent in non-supernatural belief systems. You said that a Christian who "persuades people to labor all their life in poverty and deprivation by promising them vast rewards in an afterlife" ceases to be a Christian in those actions. But if that's the case, there are a lot of false Christians we'll have to cross off the list.

Jesus himself, according to the Bible, instructed his followers to sell all their possessions, give the money away to the poor and the church, and

---

8. Jacoby, *Freethinkers*, 344.

META

spend their lives as wandering mendicant evangelists, giving no thought to what they'll eat or where they'll sleep (Matt 6:25; 19:21–24). He says that there's vast treasure laid up in heaven for those who do this.

Or what about the Roman Catholic Church? They require members of their religious orders to take lifelong vows of poverty and celibacy. If that's not a deprivation, nothing is. Would you say to them that they're not true Christians either?

Coming back to abortion, I notice that you haven't put forth your own position on the matter in detail. I'm happy to expand on the points I made last time, but I trust you'll return the favor by laying out your own views in the next installment.

You wrote:

> His "deprivation argument" claims that it's wrong to kill any human being because it deprives them of a valuable future (memories, life, experience, etc.), fetuses also have a valuable future, so killing a fetus is wrong.

This is just a different way of phrasing my previous point that human beings have a right not to be arbitrarily killed. In general, I agree with this—for example, I'd support punishment for anyone who secretly gives an abortifacient drug to a pregnant woman—but as I said, it's trumped by the bodily autonomy argument. I have the right to live, but not the right to use your body to sustain myself without your consent.

I do suggest that, if you argue fetuses have a "right to life," you should take a moment to imagine in detail what you're proposing. As an abstract principle, it sounds noble and high-minded, but the question is always: *who provides* that right? What do other people have to do or not do to permit my exercise of it?

To bring this down to the crux of the issue, a fetus can't develop into a baby without a woman's body to use as its host. And that's not a minor inconvenience, but a major burden. Even a healthy, complication-free pregnancy brings with it a whole slew of difficulties and indignities, from fatigue to morning sickness. And high-risk pregnancies can be far worse: gestational diabetes, hyperemesis gravidarum, preeclampsia, and other symptoms that range from the debilitating to the life-threatening.

I mean, just think of it. If a woman is pregnant against her will but society doesn't permit her to have an abortion, what other restrictions would have to be enforced on her for those nine months? She couldn't be permitted to drink alcohol or use most other drugs, including many prescription medicines. She couldn't be allowed to engage in many kinds of physical labor, which might mean she'd be unable to work or earn an income. She might have to be on a special diet (enforced by court order?). What else? Security guards to follow her around and make sure she was obeying doctors' orders? House arrest? Involuntary commitment?

The more you imagine, in detail, what enormous scope and horrifyingly intimate power would have to accompany a law that governs what people do with and within their own bodies, the more unsavory the prospect becomes. I don't think it's coincidental that most arguments about abortion focus on the fetus and erase the woman from the picture.

You wrote that "Fetus Adam" was "conceived by two consenting adults, knowing full well that a developing human being will/may be the consequence." The only thing that indicates consent is consent, and consent has to be given freely and renewed throughout. Just because I have sex with someone once, that doesn't mean they don't need to obtain my consent to have sex with me again any time in the future. And in the same way, consent to have sex isn't "implicit" consent to have a baby and to endure all the burdens of pregnancy.

If I cross a busy street where cars are driving back and forth, I may run the risk of being hit by a car, but that doesn't mean I *consent* to be hit by a car. (Imagine the ambulance crew saying when they find me lying in a pool of blood on the pavement, "You knew what you were getting into when you walked across Second Avenue! Don't come crying to us for help now.")

Also, since you didn't mention it, I feel that I should: as we know, not all pregnancies come about because of consensual sex. How does it change things, in your view, if a pregnancy is the result of rape?

To your point,

> If the cut-off is "conscious/thinking" and this means rational, self-reflecting beings, why does a newborn get special status if they don't qualify as such?

Just as an important clarification, I believe that what matters isn't the current existence of consciousness necessarily, but the *capability* for consciousness. If it were otherwise, it would be permissible to kill people who were deeply asleep!

We don't know what degree of consciousness a newborn infant possesses, since they can't tell us about it. That's why it's better to err on the conservative side, once we have evidence suggesting that the large-scale brain structures responsible for consciousness are functioning. In human fetal development, this seems to occur around the sixth month of pregnancy, based on medical scans that detect synchronized brain wave activity. This is about the same time as the point of outside-the-womb viability, a fortunate coincidence.

After the point of consciousness and viability, I'd still support a woman's absolute right, grounded in bodily autonomy, to end a pregnancy early. It's a safe assumption that anyone who wants to end a pregnancy so late has a good reason for it. I'd just stipulate that it can't be done through a method that destroys the fetus, if the woman's health isn't in imminent danger.

You wrote that the issue for you on this is "arbitrariness." A certain degree of judgment—arbitrariness, if you like—is inevitable in every moral decision that takes the real world into account and isn't merely based on idealized thought experiments. It's very rare that *anything* in nature comes with a convenient bright line to base our distinctions on. To avoid being pushed to one ridiculous extreme or the other, we have to draw the line somewhere, even if you could always entertain further arguments for why it should be moved in either direction.

For example, we grant people the right to vote at the age of eighteen, even though there's nothing magic or unique about that number. ("Are you really saying that a person who's seventeen years and 364 days old isn't qualified to vote, but a person who's exactly eighteen years is? That's totally arbitrary! How can we base a democracy on that?") It's a reasonable compromise given the balance of underlying rights and interests. The same is true for the age of consent for sex, the degree of consanguinity permitted in marriage, the number of consecutive terms a politician can serve, the income levels for different tax brackets, and lots of other things—they *all* involve judgment calls. Abortion isn't any different in this respect.

So, I've laid out my position. Now let's hear yours. Do you believe a single-celled embryo the size of a pinprick bears the same moral weight as an adult human being? Should a woman who unintentionally becomes pregnant be forced to bear that pregnancy against her will, even if it puts her at risk of death or grave injury?

And let me add this, because it's an important follow-up question and debates about abortion rarely address it: If you *don't* believe abortion should be legal, how would you enforce that law and what do you think the penalty should be for breaking it?

Countries like El Salvador, for example, ban abortion under all circumstances. If a woman comes to a hospital seeking medical care in the aftermath of a miscarriage, and the doctors suspect that she procured an illegal abortion, she can be arrested and confined until a forensic vagina inspector can come to perform a pelvic exam on her. Even if a woman has a nonviable ectopic pregnancy, the hospital won't do anything to help her until her Fallopian tube ruptures and the fetus dies—at which point it's a life-threatening medical emergency. Would you support anything like this?

And, it seems to me, if one's position is that an embryo or a fetus has the same moral status as an adult human, then it follows that a woman who gets an abortion should be punished with either life in prison or the death penalty, the same as any other murderer. Is that what you're advocating? If not that, then what?

ROUND 13

Metaphysics to Natural Rights and Abortion, Part III

Abortion raises subtle problems for private conscience, public policy, and constitutional law. Most of these problems are essentially philosophical, requiring a degree of clarity about basic concepts that is seldom achieved in legislative debates and letters to newspapers.[1]

—JOEL FEINBERG, *THE PROBLEM OF ABORTION*

Adam,

You put forth some great points for discussion, so let's dive right in.

Morality, Reason, and Revelation

As with my theology, the foundation of my moral philosophy is not revelation. I don't think anyone needed Moses to discern basic moral truths. Surely, one can be "good without God." Again, why accept any belief without a rational foundation? Similarly, the foundation of my moral realism is not divine command theory, but reason, specifically hylomorphism and teleology in the tradition of Aquinas and Aristotle. God is Pure Act, Being and Goodness Itself, the Final Cause and Necessity of which all contingent things depend—the source of being and goodness. You mentioned that "this sounds closer to what I would call deism than to conventional

1. Feinberg, *The Problem of Abortion*, 1.

orthodox Christianity," that the biblical God doesn't give support to the God of the philosophers, and that "an abstract principle of ultimate goodness or a transcendent Final Cause" couldn't be the God of Moses or the Christian God. You also stated that if I feel these stories are just metaphors, then I may be closer to your viewpoint than you had thought.

Two issues here. First, on metaphysics, we're nowhere close. Though we're close on practical ethics, we're on opposite ends with metaphysics, hence metaethics. Materialism rejects hylomorphism and teleology—that nature is an irreducible combination of matter and form and that all contingent things exist in between act and potency. Thus, if I were a materialist, I would not be a moral realist. Certainly, there is an *as-if-ness* to moral ontology existing in nature and we can speak of teleology heuristically, but it doesn't *actually* exist. As I've said earlier, I get moral ontology and morality being objective in a theistic or deistic worldview, but don't understand what moral ontology and objectivity is if there is no actual ground of goodness. In that vein, I agree with naturalist physicist and cosmologist Sean Carroll:

> Many (most?) naturalists have trouble letting go of the existence of objective moral truths, even if they claim to accept the idea that the natural world is all that exists. But you can't derive ought from is, so an honest naturalist will admit that our ethical principles are constructed rather than derived from nature.[2]

Second, and this goes back to faith/reason, I obviously disagree that the biblical God doesn't give support to the God of the Philosophers. In my view, God declaring "I AM" was a revelation of a metaphysical principle already conceived, albeit in a limited sense, by reason (from being, goodness, and truth to Being, Goodness, and Truth). In this moment, which is no metaphor, Moses the metaphysician became Moses the faithful in a realization that all monotheists have identified with: *Oh, it's You*. Contrary to your view, I feel that the religious revelation of "I AM" completely fits the metaphysical category of Pure Act, Being and Goodness Itself. Even further, "I AM" becomes the ultimate end of reason in the metaphysics of being. To take another line from Etienne Gilson,

> Here again historians of philosophy find themselves confronted with this to them always unpalatable fact: a nonphilsophical statement which has since become an epoch-making statement in the history of philosophy. . . . In a Christian metaphysics of being, where the supreme principle is a God whose true name is "He

---

2. Carroll, "Big Picture Part Six: Caring," PreposterousUniverse.com.

who is".... A pure act of existence... without any limitation....
The only possible explanation for the presence of such finite and
contingent beings is that they have been freely given existence by
"Him who is"....[3]

For Christians, like with Moses, the "I AM" is extended to Jesus who himself said "I AM" (John 8:58–59), that He was Truth Itself (John 18:37), and that "I and the Father are One" (John 10:30). But the metaphysician only becomes the faithful in the actual divinity and resurrection of Christ; *Oh, it's You.*

Law to Love

On Christian theology and a minimal reality check for living virtuously, we'll have to disagree. With the Christian who "persuades people to labor all their life in poverty and deprivation by promising them vast rewards in an afterlife" (your words) "ceasing to be a Christian in those actions" (my words)—I had a slave owner or human trafficker in mind (someone that claims they're a Christian but in no way does their life reflect it otherwise), but you had in mind Jesus, the very source of Christianity, and the entirety of the Catholic Church. Wow, where to begin?

For you, Christ demands stringent rules for "storing up treasures in heaven." For me, Christianity completes virtue theory—that the ultimate end of humanity is love. The "good life" now has an ultimate measure. Living only for food, lust, and material possessions is living as an animal. At the same time, religious legality, boasting, and judgement also miss the mark. The entirety of Christ's message is this: *move from law to love.*

You touched on the verses about storing treasures in heaven (Matt 6:19–20), but you should read a bit further: "For where your treasure is, there your heart will also be" (Matt 6:21). This is about a heart condition—not living only for material possessions, but living eternally and timelessly; for truth, goodness, and love. You should look at the full context. Likewise with Matthew 19, remember this was a rich man asking Jesus about the laws and good deeds he could check off the box to get into heaven. Bragging that he held to the law and good deeds, the rich man asked Jesus what else he was still missing. Knowing full well the rich man's heart condition, only then did Jesus tell him to sell his possessions and give to the poor. Therein

---

3. Gilson, *God and Philosophy*, 40–53.

lays the central message of Christianity. *There is no box you can check.* It's not about law, it's love, which sent this rich man away weeping. Contrary to your view that Christ demands everyone to give all their possessions away and live like "mendicant evangelists," the Christian message is just the opposite. Back to Matthew 22 and the greatest commandment: *loving God with all your heart and loving others as yourself.* To return to my previous quote from atheist philosopher Bryan Magee,

> God... is not in the business of awarding prizes to people who live in accordance with moral rules. You will not win any special favors from him by being virtuous.... He loves sinners just as much as he loves you.... Love is what matters, not deserving, and least of all rules. In fact, love matters about everything else. It is the ultimate reality, the true nature of existence, God.[4]

On the Catholic Church and their religious orders taking vows of poverty—do I feel that's required to be a sincere Christian? *Absolutely not.* Do I plan to tell the Catholic Church that they're not true Christians then? No, and here's why. Just as I wouldn't inform Martin Luther King's family that he wasn't a true Christian because of his adultery, neither would I inform the Catholic Church that they're not true Christians because of a certain canon. Of course, one may maintain that someone in the act of adultery is not acting as a Christian, just as one may maintain that the vows you mentioned are unbiblical. My point was on criticizing actions as unchristian, not on calling the Vatican or MLK Jr's family to tell them everything they ever did was in vain because of certain actions/canon.

Keep in mind my perspective. If you recall, I was raised Catholic, my mother is Greek Orthodox, and my in-laws are Protestants—I've been everywhere in between, including skepticism, and now ecumenically affirm the core truths of Christianity. As a Catholic, have I ever had issues with the Catholic Church? *Absolutely.* As I'm sure you're aware, many Catholics and Christians criticize the Catholic Church for the vow of celibacy and find it unchristian (and many Christians and Catholics think the Catholic Church will eventually remove such vows and allow priests to marry). But remember celibacy is only canon law, a tradition, not dogma or doctrine, one which Pope Francis has labeled "a problem" and "since it is not a dogma, the door is always open."[5] Even further, it's been reported by a close friend

---

4. Magee, *Confessions of a Philosopher*, 40, 53.
5. Jenkins, "Is Pope Francis Going to Let Priests Get Married?," ThinkProgress.org.

of Pope Francis that he finds celibacy "archaic" and plans to remove the vow of celibacy, so I wouldn't be surprised if that changed in the near future.[6]

On "poverty" and requiring "the vow of poverty," a few points of contention. Let's focus on priests for a moment. First, a point of correction: a diocese priest doesn't take a vow of poverty—he gets a nice salary, place to live, expenses, etc. Secondly, we'll disagree that the vow of poverty is life of "deprivation." Jesuit priesthood, for example, requires the vow of poverty, but they're provided a community, room and board, an allowance, etc. In many cases, they're afforded unbelievable postgraduate educational opportunities and end up as scientists, mathematicians, philosophers, theologians, teachers, etc. From a global perspective, would you label this as living a life of "deprivation"?

Abortion

I'll start with a quick layout of my position:

1. Philosophically, we should aim to legislate on universal principles.
2. Legally, everyone has the equal right to life, liberty, and pursuit of happiness (up to the point of imposing that right on "others").
3. Abortion can't be illegal (consider the case of a woman who's raped and learns she's also facing an ectopic pregnancy that threatens her life).
4. Defining "others" (personhood) at any point during the pregnancy leads to all sorts of philosophical problems.
5. Morally, abortion is not virtuous (with exceptions).

Allow me to expound, and in the process, I will address several of your questions. A key foreword, though; there are two issues at hand here: moral reasoning and legality. They are frequently conflated and I think it's important to separate "what is moral" vs. "what is legal." I noticed you jumped right in with rights, consent, and bodily autonomy. My point with Fetus Adam (conceived consensually by his parents) was to open the topic of moral possibility, not legality. You are absolutely correct that consent to have sex is not implicit consent to have a baby. If a couple found themselves in the situation of a consensual and safe pregnancy (in the first trimester),

---

6. Abigail, "Pope Francis Wants to Change Two Major Catholic Laws He Sees as 'Archaic,'" Catholic.org.

then have second thoughts later ... Now we're quickly getting into a nuanced ethical discussion. So, let's explore moral and legal possibility.

Morality

Let's begin with the scenario of "Future Land." In Future Land, imagine pro-lifers, instead of screaming picket lines, infused millions into a privately funded, special interest group called "Life and Choice" which consisted of a few main objectives: R&D for incubator technology, provisions for mothers (pre-care, procedural coverage, and post-care), and post-care funding for children.

Let's assume, with these technology advances, that viability is now five weeks. Now, instead of an abortion, "choice" and "life" are preserved by way of advanced incubator technology. Is Future Land a more moral society (both for the pro-lifers and pro-choicers)? I say yes to both. Granted, such technology is unavailable, but this highlights the issue with viability put forth in *Roe vs. Wade*. In the words of Carl Sagan and Ann Druyan, "a morality that depends on, and changes with, technology is a fragile morality; for some, it is also an unacceptable morality." Such a criteria for personhood, according to Sagan and Druyan, "puts us—like it or not—on the slippery slope." Their line of division? "The earliest onset of human thinking ... at 6 months. . . . This, it so happens, is where the Supreme Court drew it in 1973—although for completely different reasons."[7]

You mentioned that the brain structures responsible for consciousness seem to be in place around the six month of pregnancy, which is "about the same time as the point of outside-the-womb viability, a fortunate coincidence." It certainly is! You then moved to an important point, that "after the point of consciousness and viability, I'd still support a woman's absolute right, grounded in bodily autonomy, to end a pregnancy early" but you'd "stipulate that it can't be done through a method that destroys the fetus, if the woman's health isn't in imminent danger."

We agree that killing the developing fetus at this point would be a moral abomination, but a few key issues for me in your premises, first of which is ambiguity. "Consciousness," "pain," and "viability" are regularly thrown around as the magic light of moral division as if it's an all or none switch that turns on at midnight on the first day of the sixth month. Probing deeper into the neurobiology reveals this simply just isn't the case. *Pain is*

---

7. Sagan and Druyan, "Is It Possible To Be Pro-Life and Pro-Choice?," 212–14.

not consciousness and consciousness is not viability. As I mentioned earlier, we have evidence to suggest the fetus could feel pain as early as five weeks, let alone five months. At the five-month mark, if an abortion was incredibly painful for the fetus—is abortion still moral? I think you're saying that after the "Six Month Magic Light," the fetus now has consciousness, viability, and pain, so we now have a "person" (we'll get to this), but prior to that, "the fetus brain hasn't developed to the point where conscious thought or feeling is possible"—hence not a "person." Again, we'll get to consciousness and personhood, but my question at this point would be: is it pain or consciousness? They're not the same.

You clarified that "what matters isn't the current existence of consciousness necessarily, but the capability for consciousness." If that's truly the case we agree, but now you've put forward an argument in moral philosophy that posits abortion being wrong *prima facie*, from the moment of conception. In the words of philosopher Robert Larmer, "since it possesses this potential from the moment of conception, the fetus should be considered an actual person from the moment of its conception."[8] I think your "potential for consciousness" argument is framed upon having the brain architecture capable of producing consciousness (at midnight on the first day of the sixth month)? Either way, I have significant issues with the "Six Month Magic Light":

1. Scientific Accuracy
2. Ambiguity of Terms (Consciousness, Pain, Viability, Potential for Consciousness)
3. Consistency

To the first point, consciousness is commonly defined as "self-aware." Psychological and neurological tests of infants reveal self-awareness in the five-month (earliest speculation) to eighteen-month range, twelve months being the common denominator for the "mirror test" (psychology)[9] and "event related potentials" (neuroscience).[10]

To the second point, consciousness and potential for consciousness are not the same. A nine-month fetus is viable, but not conscious. A nine-month fetus can feel pain, but not be self-aware for a year after birth. The

---

8. Larmer, "Abortion, Personhood and the Potential for Consciousness," 251.
9. Amsterdam, "Mirror Self-Image Reactions Before Age Two."
10. Gabrielsen, "When Does Your Baby Become Conscious?," ScienceMag.org.

upshot is that a "Magic Light Six Month Fetus" would count as a person due to "potential for consciousness" at midnight on the first day of the sixth month—but the same fetus the day prior doesn't have a "potential for consciousness"?

To the third point, if pain is your issue, should all secular humanists be vegans/vegetarians? If consciousness is your issue, why do three-month old infants count as persons? Why is infanticide immoral? What if we could have a "better society" with the practice of infanticide, shifting resources to the needs of conscious humanity?

If one's aim is to actually probe the underlying neurobiology as well as formulate a consistent moral philosophy, it becomes apparent fairly quickly how complex this matter can get. To your question, "do you believe a single-celled embryo the size of a pinprick bears the same moral weight as an adult human being?," I think you're ultimately asking me if it's just as wrong to take an abortion pill as it is to kill an adult human. If so, my reply would be simple: Of course not. I think we'd both agree that killing an adult is more immoral, just as we would agree that killing a chimpanzee is more immoral than killing a snail (as a chimpanzee can suffer more physically/psychologically). To the topic at hand, I would hold the same logic. Infanticide would be the most immoral, partial-birth abortion right behind, late-term abortion right behind, so on so forth. Where we disagree is that abortion is wrong, period (again with exceptions) and that things get very slippery philosophically with "consciousness/pain" being the line of moral division.

Again, my points in this section have to deal with consistent moral reasoning. Certainly, not everyone is a moral realist, and for them the matter is a purely emotional and legal matter. But for the moral realist that finds themselves pregnant (leaving out cases of rape/incest/safety), consistent moral reasoning demands more than emotional and legal stakes.

Legality

On legality, we agree there has to be a division line. Of course law is somewhat arbitrary and we have to draw the line somewhere, a bare minimum of what society deems "legal" and "illegal," and a commitment by that society to enforce those laws. Supporting "a woman's absolute right, grounded in bodily autonomy" (your words) is a fair legal argument. As I stated earlier, abortion can't be illegal (I mentioned earlier the case of the raped woman with an ectopic pregnancy).

From a consequentialist view, if the abortion pill were illegal, how would a society police this logistically? With that, if early-term abortions were made illegal, and abortions now shifted to the back alley, and resources from our law enforcement agencies were allocated to abortion prevention/arrests, etc.—one could argue more death/pain/suffering would ensue. These are all fair legal, consequential, and logistical arguments to support the legality of abortion. At the same rate, the "greater good of society" arguments can (and is) used for the legality of infanticide. The dilemma with the "greater good" arguments is that they'll always be question begging—on what "good" is.

All of this bears on my original point—separating morality from legality. Of course, for moral skeptics, legality is the only matter of consideration. But for those who consider themselves moral realists, I always find it interesting the arguments put forward for *freedom to exercise rights*—then inserting ad hoc emotional/legal lines of division under the guise of rationality and moral realism. "It's legal, my right, and my choice" is certainly an accurate legal statement. But, "I'm doing this because I'm striving to be moral" seems off the mark for the moral realist. Does it not?

Metaphysics to Natural Rights and Abortion, Part III

I don't tell Father Bob how the stories about God no longer ring true, how physics and literature and music feel so much more honest than theology. I don't tell him that I've learned to be content with mystery, that the universe and its secrets excite me. I don't mention that living mindfully, trying to do good while avoiding harm, works better than keeping the Rules ever did.[11]

—MARY JOHNSON, *AN UNQUENCHABLE THIRST*

Andrew,

Thanks again for your hospitality when I came to visit Indianapolis! I relished the opportunity to go (metaphorically) into the lions' den and speak to some Christian audiences together with you. I got the impression that neither of us was precisely what the audiences were expecting, which is great! I think debates and conversations both are more interesting when they present an unusual blend of ideas and aren't just two people reciting talking points at each other.

I agree that it would be wrong to call Dr. Martin Luther King, Jr. a false Christian because of his adultery. But the difference is that King didn't *teach* adultery as permissible, he merely failed to live up to his own principles in that regard. The Catholic Church (and, as I mentioned, the New Testament itself) have always declared it a moral and positively righteous act to choose a life of deprivation in hope of an afterlife reward. You can imagine that, as an atheist, I consider it cruel to teach people to trade away their happiness in this, the only life we know *for certain* that we have, in the mere hope that there will be another one.

You wrote:

> On "poverty" and requiring "the vow of poverty," a few points of contention. Let's focus on priests for a moment. First, a point of correction: a diocese priest doesn't take a vow of poverty—he gets a nice salary, place to live, expenses, etc. Secondly, we'll disagree that the vow of poverty is a life of "deprivation." Jesuit priesthood, for example, requires the vow of poverty, but they're provided a community, room and board, an allowance, etc. In many cases, they're afforded unbelievable postgraduate educational opportunities and end up as scientists, mathematicians, philosophers,

---

11. Johnson, *An Unquenchable Thirst*, 523.

> theologians, teachers, etc. From a global perspective, would you label these folks living a life of "deprivation"?

Obviously, priests have to be fed and sheltered somehow, although I think it's overstating matters to say that they get a "nice" salary. From what I've read, despite the unique and generous tax exemptions available to clergy, most parish priests are paid little more than minimum wage. And when you consider the worldwide aging and graying of the priesthood and the tidal wave of retirements on the horizon, many of them may not get the generous pensions they were counting on.

However, the financial aspect aside, there's a deeper deprivation at work. Even more so than material wealth, which I don't think is nearly as important to happiness as most people assume, Catholic clergy are cut off by their vow of celibacy from normal human experiences like companionship, love, sex, and family. Whether it's a fixed dogma or a mere tradition, the suffering it causes in the lives of those who practice it is much the same.

My friend Mary Johnson, quoted above, who used to be a nun in Mother Teresa's Missionaries of Charity, has written about how grueling and desperately lonely her life in the order was: like a cross between prison and boot camp. She witnessed many illicit sexual relationships, and even participated in some herself.

Christianity in general and Roman Catholicism in particular has always had an uneasy, suspicious view of human sexuality. Paul wrote in one of his epistles that celibacy would be best for everyone—"it is good for a man not to touch a woman"—but marriage was a grudgingly acceptable compromise to keep people from burning in hell (1 Cor 7:1–9). Jesus strongly implied that in the afterlife, there will be no marriage and people will be sexless like angels (Matt 22:30).

To return briefly to the subject of abortion, and your point:

> Let's assume, with these technology advances, that viability is now five weeks. . . . this highlights the issue with viability put forth in *Roe vs. Wade*. To take a line from Sagan/Druyan, "a morality that depends on, and changes with, technology is a fragile morality; for some, it is also an unacceptable morality." If viability is a moving target, a more robust personhood criteria is needed.

Yes, I agree with that. Actually, your thought experiment of super-advanced incubators approaches, from the other direction, is a case that already exists today: surplus fertilized embryos produced by IVF that can be kept frozen indefinitely. If a couple chooses to implant just one of these embryos and discards the rest, are they acting immorally? Do women have a duty to implant and carry to term every single embryo that an IVF cycle produces?

I'd say no, and this tracks with my position on abortion. Regardless of what technological advances do to change the point of viability, it's consciousness, or the capacity thereof, that matters when looking at moral status. There may be marginal cases where it's hard to judge how much consciousness is present, but the evidence is unequivocal that a single-celled zygote in a petri dish doesn't and can't have the moral standing of a person. The brain architecture that makes consciousness possible just doesn't exist at that stage, or at the early stages of pregnancy in general.

This goes back to what I said last time about the law having to draw sharp lines even when nature doesn't. Obviously, there's no single moment when the "magic light" of consciousness suddenly switches on, like flipping a light switch in your living room. The emergence of characteristically human thought is a gradual process, coming as the brain develops and grows in complexity. But there still has to *be* that brain architecture in place before there's even a possibility of awareness, as opposed to mere reflex reaction. Otherwise, we end up with absurdities like a single-celled embryo having the same moral status as an adult human being.

On the topic of pain, I believe we should always strive not to inflict needless suffering. That said, I have grave doubts about "fetal pain" claims, which often emanate from anti-abortion politicians and pressure groups rather than scientists. The medical evidence suggests that perception of pain is highly unlikely before the third trimester. This is about the same time as the onset of consciousness, which isn't a coincidence.

In any case, I believe that still doesn't overrule the right of people to control their own bodies and make their own choices about whether to become parents. As I said last time, the facts are that pregnancy is often difficult, painful, and dangerous *for the woman*. At what step of our moral calculus should *that* pain be taken into consideration?

There's something else that I think, judging by your letter, we can agree on: whatever the morality of abortion, attempting to ban it outright would require an intrusive police state on a scale we can hardly imagine. I mentioned El Salvador's forensic vagina inspectors last time. Another method was Communist Romania's Decree 770, which required women to submit to mandatory state-administered pregnancy tests every month. These appalling violations of personal liberty, combined with the certainty that it would vastly increase the number of women who die from illegal self-abortions, mean that an abortion ban would do far more harm than good even if you believe that abortion is morally wrong.

Since I think we've been over this ground pretty thoroughly, I propose we broaden our focus to a larger arena, which is healthcare. Do you think the government has a role to play in providing and/or paying for healthcare for its people? How much of a role?

I'll lay my cards on the table: I believe the purpose of government is to organize and direct those collective efforts that make it possible for us to achieve things that no one could do for themselves individually. Police and military defense are part of this, protecting us from external dangers that no one could single-handedly defend against. I'd argue that the same is true of the social safety net, of which national health insurance is a key component. If it's proper for government to defend us against crime and external invasion, how can it be any less legitimate to protect us against death from disease or starvation? The latter are threats as surely as the former. What could be more "pro-life" than helping people get access to medical care they need?

As a matter of cold logistics, I don't know whether we can afford to provide fully for every medical treatment that everyone needs or might want. We only have so many doctors, so many nurses, so many hospitals. The economic evidence is unfortunately clear that when a limited resource is free, people take more than their fair share until the whole system collapses. That's the infamous "tragedy of the commons" that's tripped up so many well-meaning utopian schemes.

On the other hand, America is the richest, most technologically advanced country in the history of the world. Given these immense advantages, I think it's indisputable that we can afford to at least provide the basics—so that no one has to forsake routine medical care, and no one has to suffer or die from ailments that we can easily treat.

What often gets overlooked in American politics is that this problem has long since been solved almost everywhere in the world except here. Just about every other industrialized country has some form of national healthcare that covers more people than we do, costs its citizens less than we pay, and has better outcomes than we have. It's unconscionable how long America has refused to act on this problem, and it's even more unconscionable how bitterly and how long some social conservatives—especially those with religious motives—have fought against the only real legislative solution we've had in decades.

I think Obamacare is an imperfect solution, full of awkward, jury-rigged compromises designed to accommodate private insurance companies and other vested interests that had a stake in the health-care system as it was. Even in the best case, it's unlikely to achieve the ideal of truly universal coverage, and I can think of many further fixes it could use. But compared to the baseline scenario of doing nothing, it's a vast improvement. I have friends with chronic illnesses who've faced the threat of bankruptcy and homelessness from medical bills despite having insurance; people whose well-being was dependent in a very real and immediate sense on the law's being upheld. Anything that helps people like this makes us a more decent and humane society. As a humanist, that's something I'm all for!

ROUND 14

The Just City: Healthcare, Equal Opportunity, and the Problem of Motivation, Part I

Now it is evident that the form of government is best in which every man, whoever he is, can act best and live happily.

—ARISTOTLE, *POLITICS*

Adam,

Indianapolis was a fantastic double-header. Like you, I value a refreshing exchange of ideas and I certainly think we provided that for both audiences. To be honest, I enjoyed hanging out with you and Elizabeth more than the debates and I look forward to opportunities in the future where we can spend the weekend talking as friends, on and off the stage.

Abortion is such a complex topic. As I said earlier, I find the legal and moral arguments are frequently conflated in the discussion, so I appreciate all your insights on both components. We touched upon situations where abortion is an easy decision morally and legally. We also touched upon the greater good arguments for policing of abortive methods (from the moment of conception through late-term pregnancy) and how laws ultimately become somewhat arbitrary lines of division for the greater good of the society. All fine and good. As I said earlier, "because I can" or "it's my right" are certainly coherent legal statements.

The Just City: Part I

The obstacle that remains for me is virtue—specifically moral possibility and consistent moral reasoning. We agree on late-term abortions being immoral, but I cannot see a moral line of division in early pregnancy. Certainly, I see late-term abortions as more immoral than early-term ones. Any virtue theorist would. But then I go back to moral possibility and consistency. On fetal pain, my argument wasn't that I think pain begins in the first trimester (I don't), it's on consistency and the slippery slope; that pain, viability, and consciousness is not the same. You mentioned that you had grave doubts about fetal pain and that such claims were more driven from "anti-abortion politicians and pressure groups rather than scientists" and that medical evidence suggests "perception of pain is highly unlikely before the third trimester." As a truth seeker, *I have to agree*. In the next line, you asserted that "this is about the same time as the onset of consciousness." As a truth seeker, *I have to disagree*. As I cited earlier, consciousness as defined by the standards of neuroscience and psychology arrive five to eighteen months *after birth* (back to Singer's point, if consciousness is the bar, then infanticide is on the table). With consciousness at five-plus months after birth, pain in the late third trimester, and viability in the second trimester, you've put forward three different measures for the virtue theorist to aim at. And this virtue theorist, with consistency and moral possibility (outside certain exceptions), I don't see how one moves to abortion to be virtuous.

Speaking of complex topics—"healthcare for all" is an immensely complicated and polarizing one. To me, the underpinning that I feel is often overlooked is the balance of individual rights vs. the good of the whole. It seems it all boils down to whether healthcare is an unalienable right. Cue up the typical small government/big government discussion and away we go . . . conservatives and libertarians wonder why government should force citizens to pay for others' healthcare. Liberals wonder why we are the only industrialized nation in the world that doesn't provide some form of basic healthcare coverage to its citizens. The independent, which I am, is somewhere in between. In that vein, I agree with your sentiments:

> I think the purpose of government is to do for all of us, collectively, what we can't do for ourselves, individually. Police and military defense fall into this category, and I'd argue, so too does the social safety net, of which national health insurance is a key component. If it's proper for government to defend us against crime and external enemies, how can it be any less legitimate to protect us against death from disease or starvation? The latter are threats as surely as

the former. (What could be more "pro-life" than helping people get access to medicine they need?)

The same logic extends to public schooling. Healthcare, like education, is an obvious component for the well-being of a nation. We all support public education (whether we like or not), so why not public healthcare? Right off the bat, there are some glaring problems unique to healthcare:

1. Patient Accountability
2. Quality of US Healthcare
3. Competition for Private Health Insurance Companies
4. Public Healthcare and Fair Taxation (Back to Patient Accountability)

On the topic of patient accountability, after working in healthcare for quite some time, I'm firmly convinced that many of our nation's healthcare problems are self-induced. You typically don't "catch" Type II diabetes, heart disease, etc. Many diseases that result in billions of dollars for treatment are the consequences of the standard American diet and lifestyle.

The quality of US healthcare is also horrific. As you mentioned, from a spend to outcomes ratio, healthcare in the US is one of the worst countries in the world.

The combined effect is not healthcare, but "disease care"—patients killing themselves with their lifestyle choices and a system that treats those diseases very poorly (we certainly have some amazing medical technology and physicians, but the cost of care is outrageous). Many of our citizens don't have access to healthcare, and for those that do, US treatment costs more for a lesser outcome than in other countries.

The stage is set. Enter the sharks. It's no surprise that private health insurance companies are experiencing record profits. Besides doing everything in their power to deliberately reject claims to protect bottom lines, they also strive to remain in power. No doubt, their lobbying arms will continue to exert immense influence to remain in control and will certainly not roll over to "healthcare for all" unless they're the orchestrating middle man—more on that and Obamacare in a moment.

Now, there are certainly significant efforts in place to improve the quality of US healthcare. At the physician level, most physicians now work directly for hospitals and Uncle Sam is the biggest payer so physician/hospital accountability is undergoing a major overhaul. Quality metrics are at an all-time high and reimbursement is shifting from "cost per procedure" to bundled payment and accountable care models. The medicine of yesteryear is starting to look much different.

In response, healthcare systems are continuing to evolve. Large hospital networks are wondering why there needs to be a middle man (private insurance) and you're starting to see many "one-stop shops" where large hospital systems are becoming the insurance and treatment arm. This trend will continue to grow and the big private insurance companies will have to compete and evolve, which is a good thing. Whether or not Obama sold out to private insurers or just chose to compromise to get something off the ground goes beyond the scope of my aim here.

To get back to your question, I feel the goal to move towards "healthcare for all" is a noble one. Will it be single-payer to provide free universal healthcare, a public health insurance option (to compete with private insurance), or sticking with Obamacare (expanding Medicaid and forcing people to buy private insurance)? As with anything in life, how this will be delivered is the key. I'm in favor of every citizen being provided a basic healthcare plan. To your point, it may not be Ritz Carlton care, but it's a basic plan. Then, the private insurer would evolve into a supplemental provider. This "hybrid" or "public/private" type system is common in many other countries. If public school is provided, why not basic healthcare? Whatever direction our nation goes on this, a just "healthcare for all" system would need to address all the forementioned issues. With that, a move towards a public option would add another major issue: increased taxation. Having taxes go up to support what our nation calls "healthcare" is a scary thought.

Back to the real problem: patient accountability is the Achilles' heel. You would think if we just give people healthcare, they'll be compliant patients, make lifestyle changes, etc.—but that view is naive. Not to say there aren't extraordinary people who take advantage of opportunities they're given, but this, I argue, is the extraordinary. Let's put aside trauma and acute treatment for a moment. According to the CDC, management of chronic disease (for example heart disease, diabetes, lung disease, etc.) makes up 86 percent of our healthcare spending.[1] The idealist in me that would support education and enable universal healthcare would be the same idealist that would ask for some form of accountability. I venture to say that if patients adhered to the following sentiments—"stop smoking," "eat a high percentage plant-based diet and cut out processed foods," and "exercise frequently"—chronic disease would plummet. Say we do provide "healthcare

---

1. Centers for Disease Control and Prevention, "Chronic Disease," CDC.gov.

for all." What do we do if the real problem is patients choosing their disease states? Private healthcare, like private school, comes out of pocket. If people want to be reckless with their health on their own dimes, that is their right. Or, perhaps they're healthy, but they want boutique medicine—of course they should be afforded that right.

Towards a *just public healthcare option*, perhaps this could be a relative income/accountability based system. As we discussed, an unjust "healthcare for all" system would be one that skyrockets taxes for all citizens, yet provides substandard outcomes, while ignoring individual patient accountability. Again, patient accountability is everything. By way of example, consider four patients: Patient 1 (annual income of $45,000) Patient 2 (also $45,000), Patient 3 ($445,000) and Patient 4 ($445,000). Let's assume Patients 2 and 4 are non-smokers, have a completely healthy BMI index, and exercise regularly, while patients 1 and 3 are smokers with an out of control BMI index, high blood pressure, diabetes, and no exercise. On the income side, certain income brackets pay certain taxes for public healthcare. However, as with higher car insurance premiums for reckless drivers, I would suggest relative "base" tax increases based on one's health risk. Like a toll road: the more you use the system, the more you pay. This encourages the good of the whole, yet also individual accountability.

In short, I believe "healthcare for all" should be part of the just city, but there would need to be accountability if it were to be truly just. The public/private system, tied to outcomes and patient accountability, is the best option I see. How this is done is an immensely complex topic that I just scratched the surface on. What's your take?

The Just City: Part I

And so the children of the revolution were faced with the age-old problem: it wasn't that you had the wrong kind of government, which was obvious, but that you had the wrong kind of people.[2]

—TERRY PRATCHETT, *NIGHT WATCH*

Andrew,

I always like it when people come to our debates and tell us afterward that neither of us was who and what they were expecting. I take pleasure in confounding expectations!

I like your mention of the public school system, which is one of the best things that the government has done: a great equalizer, a stirring rod of the American melting pot, and a ladder up for children who have few opportunities—even when it's stretched thin or scapegoated by politicians, as it too often is. As I'm sure you know, there's a well-oiled campaign, backed largely by religious conservatives, to starve the public school system by allowing parents to label their tax dollars as a "voucher" that they can redirect to private, mostly religious schools. It's not hard to see how this could create a catastrophic downward spiral: the wealthiest parents pull their kids and their tax dollars out of public schools, making the schools poorer and the quality of their education worse, which leads to yet more parents pulling their kids out, which makes the schools even worse off . . . and I suspect this is precisely the intent of many of these plans.

I'm not against private schools as such, but I think there's inherent value in public schools and other public institutions that are deliberately designed to level the playing field and bring all kinds of people in contact with each other. In my view, it impoverishes us all when people retreat into their own closed-off enclaves where they can hide from differing ideas. The lifeblood of democracy, and the root of a vibrant culture, is when people from different backgrounds come in contact with each other, learn from each other, and listen to each other. It's this cross-pollination and free flow of ideas that promotes tolerance, creativity, compassion, and all the other values that are vital to a healthy and thriving democracy.

With all that said, I think that the framing of "small government" versus "big government" is a red herring. We all, liberals and conservatives

2. Pratchett, *Night Watch*, 277.

alike, cheer for government when it does things we agree with and denounce it as tyrannical when it does things we disagree with. Some of the same people who want an end to the public school system are willing to drastically expand the scope and reach of government power to put an end to abortion by passing burdensome regulations that are designed to make it impossible for family-planning clinics to operate. On the other hand, I think a lot of liberals would be happy to see spending cutbacks on the military, which is by definition the biggest and most powerful manifestation of government there is. (The oft-quoted statistic is that the US alone spends more on the military than the next seven biggest countries *combined*.) I doubt if there's anyone who's in favor of "smaller" government no matter what or "bigger" government no matter what.

This shows why it's essential, more than enshrining any specific set of political beliefs into law, to have a political system that can accommodate and channel disagreement. We all want to build the just city, but we don't all agree on what that would look like. Too often, utopian visions assume that all citizens will eagerly cooperate with each other, contribute to the common good, and work out their differences peacefully and rationally, and that's very rarely the case in reality. That's one reason why I'm in favor of capitalism, because in spite of its flaws, it's the only economic system that has an answer for the tragedy-of-the-commons problem. It's also why I'm in favor of democracy, because while it gives free rein to mob mentality and other terrible passions, it also gives people the chance to register their disagreement with the way they're being governed and demand a change of course, as opposed to totalitarian systems which have no outlet and where pressure and resentment just build up until they explode. I believe it was Winston Churchill who said that democracy is the worst form of government, except for all the others.

Countless utopian schemes have been tripped up by people just being their normal fractious, lazy, shortsighted selves. We blame outside forces for things that were under our control; we make bad decisions and then expect others to bail us out of trouble; we mindlessly sacrifice long-term well-being for transient short-term pleasure; we don't want to pay taxes, but we do want the trash pickup, paved and plowed roads, reliable utilities, good schools, and all the other services those taxes pay for. To be honest, I'm not exempting myself from this judgment! Our rationality is imperfect at best, and self-control is a finite resource that can be depleted by overuse.

Healthcare is the perfect example of this. In the Western world, we've gotten so good at fighting disease and saving people from trauma that the biggest killers are now chronic lifestyle ailments like obesity-related diabetes and cardiac disease, or cancer from smoking. And it's not just the West, either: these same ailments are skyrocketing in developing nations all around the world. It seems that when people are given the opportunity to destroy their own health, they're helpless to stop themselves. You'd think that your own long-term well-being is the best incentive there could possibly be, but it seems that most people's minds don't work that way.

I agree with you that, as much as possible, people should bear the costs of their own choices and not impose them on others. If I avoid smoking, exercise regularly, watch my diet, and so on, it would be unfair to me for my insurance premiums to go up because *other* people are being careless with their health. I like your "toll road" idea, although I'd imagine it would meet with a lot of resistance in practice. I doubt most people would be pleased by the idea of having their health regularly assessed by the government. Another possibility that would help shift the burden to the right place is to raise consumption taxes on soda, white bread, fast food, and other nutritionally worthless food products.

On the other hand, it's not enough just to talk about individual accountability. We also need to take a critical look at the culture that creates incentive structures which push people, especially poor people with fewer options, to make those bad choices.

You've heard, I'm sure, about the "food desert" phenomenon in poor neighborhoods that lack grocery stores, so the people who live there only have access to packaged, heavily processed, nutrition-poor artificial food. Food companies have spent billions of dollars to design these junk foods, carefully testing every possible combination of artificial flavors to find the exact mix that makes our taste buds go wild. They load up their products with fat, sugar, and salt, an addictive combination that appeals to primeval triggers in our brains. Alcohol and tobacco companies, too, have repeatedly been accused of crafting their advertisements to appeal to children. What better way to implant brand loyalty before people can rationally weigh the pros and cons of their choices?

Looking at it one way, you could say that people need to take more responsibility for themselves and learn to make better decisions. Looking at it another way, you could also say that advertisers spend over half a *trillion* dollars per year on advertising and marketing—mostly to advertise junk food, lifestyle drugs, unnecessary status symbols, and wasteful consumption—and they wouldn't do that if they didn't think it worked. There are whole industries of lavishly funded, highly educated professionals devoted to figuring out how to trick us into acting against our own best interests. They know what our psychological triggers and weaknesses are better than we know ourselves. What chance does the average person have against that kind of sophisticated marketing arsenal?

Why are we so easily misled into acting against our own best interests? Original sin is certainly one explanation, although you'd then have to ask why God created us with desires and dispositions he didn't want us to act on.

My explanation has more to do with the mismatch between the kind of world we live in now and the kind of world we're adapted to survive in. In the ancient wilderness where the human species evolved from apelike ancestors, life was hard, food was scarce, and survival was uncertain. Since we couldn't always predict when food would be available, the people who survived the best were the ones who had the instinct to eat as much as possible every chance they got. In our ancestral environment, bright colors, fat, sugar, and salt were the best signals of rare, valuable, calorie-dense foods. We still have that instinct, which urges us to store up fat as if we were on the African savanna and another dry season might be coming. But now we live in a world where those foods are constantly within reach. Having *too much* to eat was almost never a problem our ancestors faced, so our appetites are ill-suited to deal with it. It's no surprise that we eat ourselves sick, literally.

The point of all this is that, if we want to build a better society, we have to start by getting the incentives right. It's not enough to punish people for making bad choices; we have to make it as easy as possible for them to make *good* choices. We have to make the better options both readily available and salient. I've heard this called libertarian or soft paternalism. It's not overruling people's choices, just providing subtle, noncoercive "nudges" to steer them in the right direction.

The biggest problem is that the people who profit from the system as it is, with its screwed-up incentives, will do their utmost to resist any effort to straighten out those incentives and get them right. And those special interests are myriad: the multinational corporations that get rich by selling flavored sugar water and cigarettes; the doctors who are paid based on how many tests and procedures they perform, not on how many of their patients get well; the communities that resist efficient, high-density housing to preserve their own property values; the wealthy families that profit from tax laws that treat capital gains more favorably than labor income; the oil and gas companies that are only profitable because they don't have to pay for the pollution they create.

Fixing this goes far beyond Obamacare or any other single law or policy, and likely it can't be accomplished by top-down governance alone. Some of these problems have legislative solutions, but others don't. What do you think we can do to help people make better decisions?

ROUND 15

The Just City: Healthcare, Equal Opportunity, and the Problem of Motivation, Part II

Peter Gibbons: The thing is, Bob, it's not that I'm lazy, it's that I just don't care.
Bob Porter: Don't . . . don't care?
Peter Gibbons: It's a problem of motivation, alright? Now if I work my ass off and Initech ships a few extra units, I don't see another dime, so where's the motivation? And here's something else, Bob: I have eight different bosses right now.
Bob Slydell: I beg your pardon?
Peter Gibbons: Eight bosses.
Bob Slydell: Eight?
Peter Gibbons: Eight, Bob. So that means that when I make a mistake, I have eight different people coming by to tell me about it. That's my only real motivation is not to be hassled, that and the fear of losing my job. But you know, Bob, that will only make someone work just hard enough not to get fired.

—OFFICE SPACE

The Just City: Part II

Adam,

I agree that the typical "small government vs. big government" catchphrase is a gross over-generalization. It's polarizing and tribalistic, and distracts from some very deeper matters at hand. As you stated, "liberals and conservatives alike, we all cheer for government when it does things we agree with and denounce it as tyrannical when it does things we disagree with." I would also add independents as well. Speaking from experience, I've found that I can equally irritate liberals and conservatives.

I believe the actual debate is a deeply Aristotelian one—a difference in virtues: moral possibility, moral responsibility, and balancing individual rights vs. the good of the whole. "Well-being" and "just" can be interpreted in many ways—as you said, "we all want to see the just city, but we don't agree on what that looks like." If people can't agree on what well-being looks like, they'll certainly disagree on the role of the just city in working towards that end.

To go a little deeper than the typical labels, I find social psychologist Jonathan Haidt's research[1] to be particularly interesting about differences in virtue priorities among "conservatives" and "liberals." Haidt argues there are some common core virtues based on a few foundations: harm/care, fairness/reciprocity, in-group/loyalty, authority/respect, and purity/sanctity. The "liberal" approach is "contractual" (with primacy on harm/care and fairness/reciprocity), while the "conservative" approach is typically "beehive" (affirming harm/care and fairness/reciprocity, but also immense value of in-group/loyalty, authority/respect, and purity/sanctity). A key difficulty with rational and open-minded discord, according to Haidt, is not just differences in priorities among virtues, but the polarizing tribalism that surrounds the differences. Given humanity's history, tribalism is unsurprising, and given our nation's religious/philosophical pluralism, it should be even less surprising. In that, I feel sound reasoning (and legislation) on universal principles is the both the solution and the problem. To your point, many religious conservatives would be quite content with theocracy, something I find unconstitutional, not to mention myopic. Imagine if "Bad Religion" (not the band, just a bad religion) took control and installed their theocracy.

At the other end, many would be quite content with moral nihilism, as long as it's pragmatic and voted upon by the majority. We discussed Peter

---

1. Haidt, "Moral Psychology and the Misunderstanding of Religion," Edge.org.

Singer's views on abortion and infanticide. As humans are not "conscious" until quite some time after birth, the newborn has no natural right to life. Should the parents decide they do not want the baby, he argues it should be legal to terminate the child's life. Then, more resources could be given to conscious humanity, not all these needy newborns. Singer for President?

You made an important point:

> Some of the same people who want an end to the public school system are willing to drastically expand the scope and reach of government power to put an end to abortion by passing burdensome, intrusive regulations that are designed to make it impossible for clinics to operate.

We agree on private schools being a part of democratic freedom and that those who wish to enroll their kids in private school still need to pay equal taxation. Disallowing private schools or allowing vouchers would both be unjust in my view. Public schooling supports equal opportunity—an equal opportunity that I want for myself and my loved ones. Law enforcement is no different. For those that want to move out to the wilderness and stock up on firearms—that's certainly their legal right, but they still pay taxes for law enforcement. As with my toll road suggestion, if one only uses toll roads (hypothetically), they still have to pay taxes for public roads. On the "burdensome" and "intensive regulations" for abortion clinics, we should be careful here. One doesn't need to be religious to wish there were more "burdensome" and "intensive regulations" placed on Kermit Goshnell and similar abortion clinics. One doesn't need to be pro-life to share medical ethicist Arthur Caplan's concern (he's quite pro-choice) on Planned Parenthood's prioritization on women's health.[2] Again, universal reasoning towards just legislation is both the problem and the solution for extremism, whether it is religious fundamentalism or moral nihilism.

To the tragedy of the commons, balance of individual rights vs. the good of the whole, and science of human motivation, it sounds as if we agree that democracy/capitalism are the best possible political/economic structures to balance individual rights vs. the good of the whole while also encouraging motivation. People (in principle) have the opportunity to better their situations according to their abilities, but they also have to play according to the rules of the system that provided that opportunity (taxation for law enforcement, schooling, etc.). It would be lovely if capitalism/

---

2. Somashekhar and Paquette, "Undercover Video," WashingtonPost.com.

democracy were in a purer form in the US. Our politicians tend to sell themselves to the highest bidder, and billion-dollar industries, such as private health insurance, love to keep out competition!

That said, I think the just city should provide equal opportunity for everyone to succeed (healthcare included) and balance the individual rights vs. good of the whole. The challenge, however, goes way beyond providing opportunities—it's individuals executing upon those opportunities. Healthcare is no different. As with people taking advantage of educational opportunities, people are ultimately responsible for their own healthcare. Democracy and capitalism, in their purest form (we're definitely not there) encourages equal opportunity, but also greatly rewards those that take advantage of those opportunities. Though imperfect, I cannot think of a better duo to address the problem of motivation. It makes sense. If you want to limit motivation, offer no reward (carrot) or accountability (stick). As Ron Livingston famously stated in *Office Space*, "it's a problem of motivation."

On healthcare, I agree with you that punishment is not enough. There must be a carrot and a stick. All the while, freedom is primary. If someone is a wealthy smoker who eats four thousand calories of processed food per day—*vive la liberte!* They just don't get any carrots (say lower health insurance premiums, taxes, etc.), and only sticks (high taxation on processed foods, higher tax premiums based on their risk factors, etc.).

You mentioned that you liked my toll road idea, but you don't think people would be "pleased by the idea of having their health regularly assessed by the government." My idea is not the government assessing people's health (for example sending police officers over to people's homes for wellness checks). It would be business as usual with physicians and healthcare systems. Only now, if the government is providing healthcare, patients' data would have to be available to Uncle Sam. Like public schooling or a public defender, if you cannot afford any other option, you need to play within the rules of what is provided. Demanding healthcare for every patient, without patient accountability, carrots/sticks, will just bankrupt the system.

Here's what I see as the overarching problem. "Healthcare for all" is a lot like "well-being"—the devil is in the details and there will surely be disagreement on what this looks like. Free universal healthcare, if that's what we're talking about (as opposed to a "government option"), would be a massive undertaking—not just tax increases on processed foods, but tax increases on all individuals. We both agree that two individuals of the same income but wildly different lifestyle choices should not incur the same financial burden (let's say Person A is extremely healthy and Person B eats four thousand calories per day of processed food, chain smokes, and never exercises). Something would be awry if they both had the same tax increase. For the wealthy that want to eat, drink, and smoke themselves into diabetes and heart failure, they pay extra on the taxes assessed by their habits, supplemental private insurance, pay out of pocket for their choices, higher taxes on their risk factor (if a toll road-type system were enacted), etc. For those at the poverty level and low income, things get tricky. We need to try to provide an opportunity for them to make good decisions.

To the point you raised on how we can help people make better decisions—now that's the million-dollar question! In my humble opinion, it would take a major overhaul at the political, grassroots, and individual levels to allow the realization of human health. I don't think anyone would disagree that knowledge is power and that the right incentives will influence motivation.

At the political level, the game is fixed. Higher costs/taxes on processed foods Mr. Processed Food Lobbyist? *Over his dead body*. Competition (universal healthcare, single payer, government option, etc.) Mrs. Private Health Insurance Lobbyist? *Over her dead body*. Challenge the food and private medical insurance industries, Mr. and Mrs. Politician? *Over their dead bodies*. Something seems inherently wrong with our government subsidizing processed foods that kill its citizens—which is in direct conflict with minimizing disease incidence and healthcare costs—which ensures record profits to private health insurance companies. It's a vicious cycle—just follow the money and power. I find it fascinating that physicians now have potential conflicts of interest up on the Internet for public record, but politicians need not be transparent. Our nation deciding that the health of their citizens is key, as opposed to lining the pockets of industry, lobbyists, and politicians. The problem is those in power love the system the way it is so their pockets get continually lined. Legislating the right incentives towards human health is both the solution and the problem.

The grassroots level has been encouraging. I'd love to see this increase. In terms of speed and effectiveness, it's extremely powerful to have individuals and communities come together to put creative programs in place to allow folks at the low income and poverty level to get life-sustaining foods for less than processed foods. One thought would be expanding upon government subsidized urban farmers market programs where not only jobs could be created, but plant-based foods are provided for less than processed foods (this will be greatly limited by former issue). Perhaps, there could be attached Wellness Centers where folks can exercise, get life coaching, nutritional counseling, primary care, etc. If not driven directly by the government, I've seen foundations that are part of private enterprises provide healthy food to those in economic crisis. Things like this are a tremendous win-win for profitable businesses and those in need, a tax write-off that is actually going to good use. Efforts such as these are key. Grassroots change my friend—from the political level to the local level to the individual and vice versa. This is a mountain to climb, but so was (and still is) equality of race and gender.

Focusing solely at the individual level reveals the largest issue at hand. As you eloquently stated, "it seems that when people are given the opportunity to destroy their own health, they're helpless to stop themselves." Many of us know exactly what we need to do to be healthy, but do the opposite. Back to the problem of motivation. Education and enabling people to make better decisions only goes so far. Social change—let's say wellness centers and cheap plant-based foods are put on the corner block—again only goes so far. Carrot and stick will certainly motivate but would be unjust unless major social change and educational programs are put in place to allow people the means to make good decisions. But even if all these measures are in place—even if we achieve the just city—people are people. The ultimate answer I think lies with the individual, in caring about yourself enough to care (as well as others in not burdening them with your health decisions).

What a just "healthcare for all" picture looks like is an immensely difficult topic. I think it's a combination of providing opportunity (education, social change, etc.) and encouraging motivation (carrot/stick). And just like "well-being," the exact make up of what "healthcare for all" with a balance of individual rights and good of the whole is difficult to say. And as with defining "the just city," the devil is in the details.

META

Thirty-seven years ago, that subordination so dear to the patriarchal heart came within a hairsbreadth of ending my life. And my heart, in the thirty-seven years since, has wanted to break each time I ponder how many lives it did end.[3]

—SHERRY MATULIS

Andrew,

I think Haidt's insight about the five foundations of morality has a lot of validity, although I'd argue that the conservative, "beehive" values tend to work better in smaller and more homogeneous societies. Large, multicultural civilizations, by their nature, need to rely first and foremost on the "contractual" values of harm/care and fairness/reciprocity to mediate clashes of interest. Those are the "common currencies" that all human beings share and largely agree on, whereas beliefs about who constitutes the in-group, which are the authorities who should be respected, and what acts are sacred or taboo all vary enormously among cultures.

I'd also suggest that in-group/loyalty, authority/respect, and purity/sanctity are the moral principles of scarcity. If you're a tribe of hunter-gatherers surrounded by hostile rivals, or a village of subsistence farmers dependent on the weather, there really is a need for people to pull together and sacrifice for the sake of survival. Under those circumstances, there isn't a lot of room for people to go their own way and do their own thing.

Luckily, we've grown past that need! Compared to past eras, the society you and I live in is one of immense abundance. As I said last time, one of our biggest health problems is that we're surrounded by *too much* food—a problem that, until just a few generations ago, our ancestors would have found incomprehensible. The average middle-class person today can buy any kind of food they want, in any quantity, from anywhere in the world, no matter the season; can heat their home in winter or cool it in summer to any temperature they desire; can travel virtually anywhere on the planet in a few hours' time; can access any kind of information from the entire collective repository of human knowledge on command. Not even kings or emperors of a few hundred years ago could have commanded such luxuries.

---

3. Matulis, "How I Earned My Feminist Credentials," 543.

The Just City: Part II

    Along with that historically unparalleled abundance, we also—that is to say, you, me and most likely the people reading this book—enjoy vastly expanded freedom to think, believe, and speak as we see fit. That, too, is new and unprecedented—the idea that truth is something to be discovered through free debate and mutual persuasion, rather than something handed down by unchallengeable tradition or established by the decrees of kings and priests.

    I don't think it's a coincidence that material wealth and intellectual freedom advance hand in hand. Rather, each one promotes and nurtures the other, in an accelerating upward spiral of progress. We're unbelievably fortunate to have been born into a time where there's room for individuality, for experimentation, and for marching to the beat of your own drum. And that's fortunate, because I think the best society is the one that gives people the greatest possible freedom to seek out their own vision of the good life, so long as it doesn't interfere with others doing the same. Who could disagree with that?

    On that note, let me offer a few closing thoughts on choice. While I personally believe abortion should be legal, I recognize that a lot of people don't feel the same way I do, and so there is—there has to be—space to debate it. I'll never object to people stating their opinions honestly and without pretense. However, what I see more and more in conservative states is a backdoor attempt to ban abortion by burdening women and clinics with ever-greater and more onerous regulation, while claiming it's all about concern for women's health. (There are already vast swathes of red states, Texas in particular, where there simply are no clinics within hundreds of miles.) This, in my opinion, demonstrates transparent bad faith.

    You decry ghastly, bottom-feeder quacks like Kermit Gosnell, and you're right to do so. But Gosnell isn't an example of what happens when abortion is under-regulated. He's an example of what happens when abortion is *over-regulated*, to the point of being impossible to obtain legitimately. If we go much further down this path, we'll see a return to the bad old days of back alleys, coat hangers and women dying of hemorrhage. It's already happening in some places, and it could well get worse.

    If you care about women's health, the way to prove it is by ensuring that women have the ability to take care of themselves—or as you put it, "allow them the means to make good decisions." Whatever your feelings on the matter, it's no coincidence that the vast majority of people opposed to legal abortion are also opposed to comprehensive sex education, access to contraception, and even paid family leave—the very things that make it possible to make responsible decisions about sex and pregnancy. The policies being pushed by these prudish religious fundamentalists aren't intended to safeguard anyone's life or health, but to punish people, especially women, for having unapproved sex.

And it's not hard to see where this idea comes from. Misogynistic fear and loathing of women's sexuality is a prominent and obvious theme in many holy books, including the Bible. Virtually without exception, women in Scripture are either chaste virgins, modest wives, or else evil temptresses, prostitutes, and Jezebels. Just look at the Old Testament passages that say that a woman who gives birth to a daughter is ritually unclean for twice as long as a woman who gives birth to a son (Lev 12:1–5). The New Testament isn't any better: it blames the downfall of humanity on a woman tempting a man, and commands that women can be saved only if they keep quiet, obey the commands of men, and subserviently bear children (1 Tim 2:11–15). Two millennia of virulent sexism and the systematic exclusion of women from every position of religious or political power have come from passages like this. The way I see it, religious authorities have a long list of wrongs to answer for before they ever again have the presumption to tell women what is or isn't necessary for their health.

It sets a bad precedent, too, if the state can use regulation to harass something into nonexistence that it would be illegal to ban outright. Just imagine if the government wielded that same tactic against churches!

Imagine the burdens we could put on religion with a slow drip-feed of one burdensome law after another. We could have mandatory, state-imposed waiting periods and in-person counseling sessions from an atheist before someone could attend church. We could have laws that allow people to sue their pastors if they don't feel a sense of inner peace and fulfillment. We could have government-written scripts that the minister was forced to read before every service ("Warning! The government has determined that belief in the contents of this sermon may endanger your life, health, and ability to think critically"). Imagine if you had to travel hundreds of miles and take time off work and find childcare just to attend the church of your choice.

This gets to the point about the supposed inefficiency of government. The fact is that government is often very efficient at doing what it sets out to do, which isn't always what the stated purpose of a law is.

When you see a law or a rule that seems ridiculous, needlessly complex, or riddled with giveaways or loopholes, it's rarely because politicians are idiots who can't just write a bill that says what they mean. It's more often because some high-powered corporate lobby or political pressure group is demanding it for their own purposes. (One of my favorite examples: one of the major lobbies opposing simplification of the tax code are the accounting firms that sell tax-preparation software.)

This gets at one of the bigger problems with democracy, which is that a shockingly large number of people don't watch the news, don't pay attention, don't vote—or if they do vote, it's based on the most superficial of generalities, like which candidate is more attractive or seems more confident. That means that laws often get made by the relatively small number of people who do care and do show up, both for better and for worse.

There's an inherent collective-action problem here. If a law will cost me and everyone else fifty cents a year in extra taxes, I won't have a strong motivation to care about that trivial sum. But if all those pennies flow to one company, for them it's 150 million dollars a year, and you can bet they'll fight with everything they have to get it passed!

If there's anything that's the flaw in our political system, it's this. It's too easy for pressure groups, be they corporate or religious, to capture the loyalty of politicians and influence laws in ways that are detrimental to everyone else. James Madison wrote about his hope that differing factions would balance each other out and prevent this outcome, but history shows that that rarely works out as well as we might hope.

Whether this is a solvable problem, I don't know. We can both agree, I'm sure, that the First Amendment and its wall of separation between church and state has largely prevented one kind of societal capture by pressure groups, namely theocracy. But that's just one instance of a much bigger general problem.

I also don't think that just "making government smaller" is a blanket fix to the problem, as many libertarians would postulate. It does have a simple, intuitive appeal: the government does bad things, so let's make it smaller and less powerful and it will do less of those bad things. The problem with that, as I see it, is that if it's not a democratically-elected government making the rules, it will be someone else we may like even less. Even in a theoretically minimal state, there are so many ways to coerce others to your will.

Too many people have forgotten, or never read about, the bad old days when workers had to go work in company towns where they lived in company dorms and were paid in scrip currency that was only good at the company store. If they displeased the boss, they could lose their savings, their job, and their home all in the same day. And even if that threat wasn't enough to keep them from agitating for better working conditions, the company owners could always hire private goon squads to crack some heads or even murder the troublemakers. Who's going to prosecute, after all, in a country with no red-tape labor laws and a weak, hands-off government?

I don't have any easy answers to offer for what we should do instead. In fact, I'm more suspicious of reductive utopian plans that try to distill all the complexity of human behavior into just a few principles. (Wasn't it H. L. Mencken who said that every problem has a solution that's neat, simple, and wrong?)

I'm inclined to think that there's ultimately no substitute for an informed and politically engaged citizenry, even if that will always be more of an ideal than a reality. At the very least, this argues for a robust public education system and a vigorous free press. But this analysis suggests another possible answer: perhaps reducing inequality may be a good thing for its own sake. A more sharply progressive income tax would be one way to do it. What if we brought back the 90 percent top tax bracket of the Eisenhower era?

I'm not saying there should be perfect equality of outcome, because people do need a motivation to work and to strive. We should give everyone an incentive to contribute to society using whatever talents or skills they have. But it's plausible that allowing any one individual or group to accumulate too much wealth and power, relative to everyone else, is harmful to democracy. It gives them the ability to sway the democratic process toward unjust outcomes.

The one-person, one-vote principle of democracy is a check on excessive personal ambition and too-radical change. It requires people to compromise and build consensus rather than to impose their will on others. Maybe that's a moral principle we should consider extending beyond just the ballot box, and try building a society where everyone has a real and meaningful voice in how they're treated and what the laws should be. That could well be the path toward a better and more just world for everyone, regardless of whether you're atheist or theist, male or female, or any other distinction you'd care to name. I admit it's a bold speculation, but I think it's one that's worth exploring!

ROUND 16

Closing Statements

Even if there is only one possible unified theory, it is just a set of rules and equations. What is it that breathes fire into the equations and makes a universe for them to describe? The usual approach of science of constructing a mathematical model cannot answer the questions of why there should be a universe for the model to describe. Why does the universe go to all the bother of existing? Is the unified theory so compelling that it brings about its own existence?[1]

—STEPHEN HAWKING

Adam,

How does one eloquently close fifteen rounds of back and forth on God, the big questions, and the just city? This has no doubt been the most fruitful and illuminating exchange I've had on such matters with someone of opposing views (though on many things we do agree). Prior to providing some closing thoughts, you brought up some important points on misogyny. As fellow truth seekers, we agree this is an immense problem.

The Bible verses you mentioned certainly bear pause, but biblical literalism/inerrancy/interpretation is an entire exchange itself—and one usually debated intra-Christianity! Though this topic falls outside the scope of our dialogue, I think non-misogynistic Christians (I trust we'd agree there's a few out there!) can go two ways. Many reject biblical literalism/

---

1. Hawking, *A Brief History of Time*, 190.

inerrancy; others with a lean towards biblical literalism/inerrancy argue that the whole of the New Testament and Christian message portrays an entirely different picture that affirms the intrinsic value of every person and equality of women.

The unfortunate reality is that sexism, misogyny, and bigotry has a past, present, and future in religious circles. Following your blog, I think we'd agree the same is true for the irreligious. Tribalism, fanaticism, and nihilism will always peek their ugly heads. Sexists, misogynists, and bigots will continue to justify their behavior, whatever their metaphysics and a/ theology may be.

This goes back to our core agreement on democracy—justice demands universal reasoning. It also highlights an important difference between morality and legality. What is legal says nothing about what is just. Democratic law is ultimately arbitrary and simply the vote of the majority, which we've both agreed has tremendous imperfections, biases, and power grabs. Unsurprisingly, we disagree on the metaphysics. For me, moral truth, like mathematical truth, is discovered. *Telos* (inherent goals and value intrinsic to nature) and goodness are very real features of reality—not just "made up," culturally relative, or voted on by the majority. With materialism, I don't understand what "just," "good," or "moral" means beyond preference or vote (more on that in a moment).

One topic we discussed along these lines was abortion. I tried to simplify the discussion by separating morality from legality and providing what I believe to be a modest hypothesis—that abortion isn't virtuous and only gets more immoral the further along the pregnancy goes. One doesn't need to espouse theism to arrive at this view and I provided some secular arguments in support of this position (the late Christopher Hitchens, my personal favorite of the "New Atheists," held this view). At the same time, I offered certain situations where abortion is not immoral as well as my admission that I don't see how a society could make it completely illegal (we discussed the absurdities of house visits for pelvic exams, policing for the abortion pill, etc.).

If our aim is a just society, we agree that separation of church and state is an absolute necessity, along with unbiased press, strong public education, and some form of healthcare for every citizen. At the same rate, I believe the just city is one that supports equal opportunity, while balancing the problem of motivation (with accountability, carrots, sticks, etc.). At the one end, the game being fixed by the powerfully corrupt is unjust. At the other, forced equal distribution of resources is also unjust. At the end of the day, I don't see a better system than democracy and capitalism to address the problem of motivation. A purer democratic and capitalistic society seems to be the answer. What that looks like exactly, I do not know.

Allow me to close on theology/metaphysics by first providing my sincere thanks. I already had my doubts, so spending time with you more than helped perk up my inner skeptic! Thank you for opening my eyes to another perspective and moving me to reconsider some of my own views. You helped me tear down some conceptual idols, shift on some views, and mature in others. You also helped me affirm my passionate rejection of any mechanistic, deistic god, being among beings (as Etienne Gilson labels the "watchmaker of Voltaire" and the "carpenter of cheap apologetics")[2] as well as "Christendom" Christianity (what Kierkegaard criticized as a dispassionate, judgmental, and hypocritical cultural theocracy)—in Gandhi's words, "so many of you Christians are so unlike your Christ."[3] God, "I AM," *Ipsum Esse Subsistens* (Subsistent Being Itself), and discipleship Christianity—passionate, humble, charitable, Christ-following Christianity—is all that remains as the ultimate ideal.

I think the main theme underpinning our exchange has ultimately been about the big questions and the metaphysics within our respective worldviews. For truth seekers, "theism" or "atheism" is not the end of the conversation, just the beginning. Why? What kind? How do the big questions fit into that worldview? "This is my worldview"—yawn. "This is my metaphysics of being"—now we're cooking! Hawking's quote above is ultimately a restatement of Leibniz's timeless question, "Why is there something rather than nothing?" This question, along with "Is morality objective and how?," "Is there such thing as free will?," and "Is mathematics invented or discovered?" are just a few deep metaphysical questions we've wrestled with throughout our exchange. On God's existence, free will, morality, and consciousness, I'm a realist. To be more specific, I'm an Aristotelian realist of which theism is reason's end.

On one hand, I understand the appeal of naturalism. Matter is no doubt a very real and obvious part of reality—a separate material/immaterial Platonic metaphysic seems far out—yet matter being the entirety of reality also bears pause. To me, hylomorphism and teleology is an unmatched metaphysics. Plato's timeless idea grants the immaterial ontology (but adds

---

2. Gilson, *God and Philosophy*, 142.
3. Basebang, "Gandhi's Message to Christians," MKGhandi.org.

a host of other philosophical problems) while Democritus's attempts to simplify the philosophical problems by reducing everything to "just matter" (killing immaterial ontology, formal/final causes, and creating all sorts of other philosophical problems).

In the shortcomings of Plato and Democritus, I see the genius of Aristotle—that all contingent things are an irreducible composite of matter and form. Things like causation, value, and mathematical ontology are intrinsic to matter. The cosmos is a composite physical and immaterial mathematical reality; humans are a composite body and immaterial "I"—all things are irreducible composites of physical and immaterial intrinsic ontological properties. In such a metaphysics of being lie ontological categories such as being/nonbeing and act/potency (for things that have being). At first blush, this may sound bland or irrelevant, but when applied to the big questions, it's unsurpassed. The universe and everything within it seems contingent and constantly changing. From quantum mechanics to morality, all contingent things seem to exist between act and potency. Humans, the social-rational animal have a certain potential, given our nature—conscious, free, and moral capabilities—"well-being" is simply actualizing upon these potencies to a certain degree. Because anything exists, because there is goodness, there is a Source.

To be clear, I'm not arguing "because I don't have an explanation, God exists." As an engineer, philosopher, and empiricist, I'm not particularly persuaded by "god of the gaps" arguments. My argument is not one of empirical ignorance, but of philosophical inference to the best explanation from what we know most intimately (being and nonbeing, consciousness, free will, morality, intrinsic value)—to ontological Aristotelian-Thomistic concepts like form/matter, act/potency, formal and final causation. For a realist, God is metaphysically inferred analytically—being to Being, goodness to Goodness, contingent to Necessary, change to the Unchanged—as reason's end. In Aquinas's words, "we call this God." God is Goodness and Being Itself, Pure Act, the Necessary and sustaining source of which all contingent things depend. This "God of the Philosophers" is not just discovered rationally (albeit finitely and in a very limited sense), but spiritually as well. Back to neuroscientist Andrew Newberg's research—we're all metaphysicians and mystics to some degree—we can't help it. This sense of divine, rational/metaphysical and mystical/spiritual, to me imparts ontology.

My main issue with naturalism is not that it's anti-theism, but what generally comes with the overarching metaphysics of materialism on being;

and, from that, what I believe to be an insurmountable challenge in preserving realism—for morality, consciousness, and free will—in any meaningful sense. Naturalism posits matter as the source of its own existence, maintaining an infinite regress, and rejects our faulty metaphysical/religious cognitive architecture as illusory, simply an evolutionary byproduct that was passed on due to selective fitness. Back to Dawkins:

> It's a universe of electrons and selfish genes, blind physical forces and genetic replication. . . . No purpose, no evil and no good. Nothing but blind pitiless indifference . . . DNA neither knows nor cares. DNA just is, and we dance to its music.[4]

The consequence, as Dawkins readily admits, is that moral abominations like rape are completely arbitrary, simply a sociobiological taboo—they could have just as easily been positively selected from our evolutionary past as good.[5] And so we come upon the finale of naturalism—our suggestive religious and metaphysical minds point not at Being and Goodness Itself, but selfish genes. But we want to have our metaphysical cake and eat it too, so we look for it in matter—for why anything exists at all—for meaning, conscious agency, morality, and free will. But there is no *telos*, formal/final causes, or intrinsic value in a materialistic universe—"only atoms and the void" (Democritus).

I've seen naturalists approach this dilemma in a few different ways.

I Don't Want to Talk About It Naturalists like Lawrence Krauss have only ignorance and contempt for the big questions, so they attack straw men, avoid the question, or fallaciously redefine the word "nothing" to address the "Why is there something rather nothing?" question.

Bait and Switch Naturalists like Sam Harris attempt to defend realism and naturalism, reject a Platonic realm or teleology (as I feel a good naturalist should), but then play word games that science provides objective right/wrong answers to moral questions.[6] The issue here is conflating is/ought, fact/value, method/metaphysics, epistemology/ontology—smuggling teleology in the back door—grabbing the benefit of Aristotle's hylomorphism heuristically, but rejecting it ontologically. Again, we all want to have our metaphysical cake and eat it too, but the problem for such a virtue ethic

---

4. Dawkins, *River Out of Eden*, 133.
5. Dawkins, Interview with Justin Brierley, PremierChristianRadio.com.
6. Harris, *The Moral Landscape*.

(virtue without ontology/teleology) is that it ceases to be a virtue ethic and amounts to the following description: *subjectivism*.

Not Too Natural Naturalists like Roger Penrose, Max Tegmark, and Thomas Nagel realize the dilemma, but refuse to smuggle in ontology in the Sam Harris-esque fashion, so they posit Platonic realities (Penrose and Tegmark) or an undiscovered natural teleology (Nagel) to make room for metaphysics (mathematical ontology, fine tuning, teleology, consciousness, free will, rationality, morality, etc.).[7]

Bite the Bullet Naturalists like Alex Rosenberg, Jerry Coyne, and Peter Singer throw the ontological baby out with the bath water, holding that naturalism requires rejecting odd metaphysical entities like free will, purpose, meaning, objective morality, etc.[8] We are, in Singer's words, "free to choose who we are to be. . . . We have no essential nature. . . . We simply exist and the rest is up to us."[9] Of course, we should choose to be moral ("whatever the cause of our choices"), living according to Singer's postulates because we'll find life "more fulfilling" and "contribute to making the world a better place."[10] What "moral," "a better place," or "free to choose" means in a purposeless and metaphysically bankrupt existence (where the cause of our choices is selfish genes dancing to DNA) means in such a view—I just can't follow.

In the end, a speculative metaphysics is imparted on everyone to reason, as best we can, to the ultimate nature of reality. In that, my thesis ultimately remains unchanged. I see both of our worldviews as religious. If you recall my definition of faith, it ultimately amounts to *trust*. In this case, trust that our specific metaphysical picture of reality is the right one. For many theists and atheists, this bar is low. Reasoned metaphysics is the furthest thing from their minds. Trust is given blindly and tribally—they ask us to accept their positions because the Bible says so or Dawkins says so. As with you, my bar is high. I can only embrace a faith that has earned my trust with a sound metaphysical and rational foundation.

Your faith lies in materialism and secular humanism; mine in hylomorphism and theism. Doubtful, I am, that Democritus's materialism can earn my trust on the big questions. With that, the leap of faith from materialism to secular humanism is too much to bear. And please don't

---

7. Nagel, *Mind and Cosmos*.
8. Singer, *How Are We to Live?*
9. Ibid, 5.
10. Singer et al., "Peter Singer: You Ask the Questions," Independent.co.uk

misunderstand me; it's not that I don't find secular humanism inspiring. The language is incredibly moving. Actually, I think Ursula Goodenough labels it best in describing humanism as a "religious naturalism" in which humans are "inherently sacred"—a "faith" she professes on the "continuation of life" being its own "sacred circle that requires no further justification . . . no purpose other than that the continuation continue until the sun collapses or the final meteor collides."[11] As a fellow theologian, all existence being inherently sacred is a shared sentiment, but as a philosopher, on what rational grounds does such a faith stand? I, along with *Bite the Bullet Naturalists*, have to audit such teleology (morality, free will, meaning, and purpose) as disallowed from the toolbox of materialism. In that, it's not that I take issue with many of the practical aims of such a "religious naturalism"; it's the underlying metaphysics. If faith be the destination (and I argue it is for anyone who trusts in their specific worldview), I find Being Itself, not matter itself, a more reasonable path to being, goodness, and purpose.

There you have it. Though we ended up in different places, I tip my hat to you as a fellow truth seeker. I remain incredibly enthused at our common ground, on affirming the intrinsic value of all humanity, and on taking action to make this world a better place. Even more, I've made a true friend. And we can stand together as friends and change the world—uniting to fight against injustices like poverty and human trafficking. We'll debate on the metaphysics on the car ride over.

Your friend,
Andrew

---

11. Goodenough, *The Sacred Depths of Nature*, 59, 171–74.

META

no use to make any philosophies here:
    I see no
god in the holly, hear no song from
the snowbroken weeds: Hegel is not the winter
yellow in the pines: the sunlight has never
heard of trees: surrendered self among
    unwelcoming forms: stranger,
hoist your burdens, get on down the road.[12]

—A. R. AMMONS, "GRAVELLY RUN"

Andrew,

    Well, we've been up one side and down the other—from the origins of the universe to the nitty-gritty of American constitutional law and back again. It's fitting, as this extended dialogue draws to a close, that we revisit some of our starting points.

    After all this time, our biggest point of contention still seems to be the ontology of morality and whether right or wrong can be "real" in a godless universe. It's ironic to me that we can differ on this most fundamental point while agreeing on so much else of considerably lesser philosophical significance.

    I've sometimes called this the "standing on air" phenomenon, in reference to the fact that to a theist who believes morality consists of obeying God's will, seeing an atheist be moral without that supernatural foundation can be a disconcerting, even frightening experience—like seeing someone standing on thin air with no visible means of support. They believe that if they were in that position, they'd come tumbling down, and they can't see why we don't. More than once, I've had the bizarre experience of religious proselytizers arguing with me that because I'm an atheist, I shouldn't care about right or wrong. In other words, they're trying to convince me to be more evil!

    The truth is that atheists do have an objective foundation for morality. It's just a different kind of foundation from the one most religious believers are used to, and if you don't know what to look for, it's invisible. (Remember

---

12. Ammons, "Gravelly Run," 11.

the famous scene in *Indiana Jones and the Last Crusade* with the bridge that you can't see unless you're looking at it from precisely the right angle?) It's the recognition that happiness matters, that it's the goal of all our strivings, and that the ways to create it are neither arbitrary nor unknowable, but grounded in factual truths about the kind of beings we are.

Now, I grant that the laws of morality are different from the laws of nature, in that nothing *enforces* them. It's true that there's no right or wrong woven into the foundation of the universe. The laws of atomic physics don't care whether we use them to build nuclear reactors that supply heat, light and power to millions of people, or nuclear missiles that annihilate cities. The mathematics works the same either way.

Nevertheless, I maintain that my search for truth has helped bring me to a deeper understanding of right or wrong. That's not because a god is hiding under the laws of physics, but because pondering the *deepest* questions will inevitably give you a jolt of perspective that makes our similarities loom much larger than our differences. When I come face to face with how fragile we are, how small, it fills me with a fierce love of humanity, an admiration of what we're capable of, and a redoubled resolve to be kinder to each other and to the world that is our home.

Carl Sagan said it best in his "Pale Blue Dot" speech:

> The Earth is a very small stage in a vast cosmic arena. Think of the endless cruelties visited by the inhabitants of one corner of this pixel on the scarcely distinguishable inhabitants of some other corner, how frequent their misunderstandings, how eager they are to kill one another, how fervent their hatreds. Think of the rivers of blood spilled by all those generals and emperors so that, in glory and triumph, they could become the momentary masters of a fraction of a dot.[13]

Think of what it would mean—what it would *really* mean—to see existence through an atheist's eyes. We find ourselves alone in this vast, bewildering, implacable universe, with no hint that a higher power watches over our lives or that a messiah will come down from the clouds to rescue us. If we stumble, no one will pick us up. If we destroy ourselves, the curtain will fall and that will be the end. As you put it, there's nothing at the bottom but "blind pitiless indifference."

But does that make our lives illusory, our struggles futile, our existence meaningless? Not at all! In fact, it means the precise opposite: it means that

---

13. Sagan, *Pale Blue Dot*, 8.

it's all the more urgent, all the more desperately important, that *we* care for each other, that *we* learn wisdom, that *we* build just and peaceful societies. It's all up to us, and we can't evade the responsibility: to fill this one small corner of the cosmos with light, love, and laughter; to live fearlessly and fully, and as best we can, to bring happiness to our fellow creatures. We are the makers of meaning, we are the ones who matter, and the purpose we have is whatever we choose for ourselves.

Is this all "illusory"? Not as far as I'm concerned. But if you're stuck on the idea that this vision is insufficient somehow, that it's lacking a certain metaphysical *je ne sais quoi*, let me offer some unlikely words of wisdom. The author Robert E. Howard said it best, in the words of his classic pulp hero Conan the Barbarian:

> Let teachers and priests and philosophers brood over questions of reality and illusion. I know this: if life is illusion, then I am no less an illusion, and being thus, the illusion is real to me.[14]

The funny thing is, I see it almost the opposite way from how you do. If an all-powerful creator planned the cosmos from start to finish, then there *can't* be free will or meaningful choice. If we have no power to change the divine plan, then we're no more than puppets, or characters in a play, or a lab rat running a maze at the behest of an experimenter: the outcome is decided for us, whatever freedom we may think we have. I think it makes our existence *more* real and meaningful to know that our lives, our choices, our struggles are entirely our own, and the responsibility is ours as well.

When I look at the world's holy books and religious traditions, what I see is a strange alloy. There's beautiful poetry there, yes, and enduring myths and wildly imaginative cosmologies and time-tested maxims, but it's mixed together with crushing ignorance, benighted superstition, and appalling cruelty. The sheerest absurdities are asserted with total confidence, and rival sects fight literally to the death over the tiniest iota of interpretation.

There are wise, humane believers, I know. (I've met one of them in this exchange.) There are also those who claim an allegedly superior understanding of God's will, and use it to justify their beliefs about whom we should hate, whom we should oppress, and whose blood we should spill.

But that's just the point: religion isn't something handed down to us from above. It's a thoroughly human phenomenon, built on our dreams and our desires, and as such it carries within itself the seed of all the good and

---

14. Howard, "Queen of the Black Coast."

all the evil that human beings are capable of. The same is true of atheists, of course—we're just as human as anyone else, and just as fallible. But the fact that religious beliefs are built on these unchanging relics of the past, these archaic directives literally hewn into stone, makes them particularly resistant to moral progress and correction. You may view God in a highly abstract and ineffable way, as the philosophers' ultimate ground of being and goodness, but billions of people still imagine him in jarringly literal terms, as a cosmic landlord who cares above all else about which words we use to praise him, how we dress, what foods we eat on which days, or what kinds of sex we have.

To bring this back to the second half of our debate: given the enormous diversity of humanity and our vast potential for both good and evil, designing the ideal society is a formidable challenge. It can neither be so rigid and dogmatic that one person's vision is enshrined into law and everyone else's is crushed out—that way lies tyranny—nor can it be so permissive or minimal that no one holds sway and everything goes—that way lies chaos. It's our collective responsibility as human beings to steer the ship of society between these two treacherous shoals.

We'll probably never reach unanimous agreement about everything, nor is it necessary. What we can agree on, I hope, is that the purpose of civilization and governance is to make it possible for everyone to pursue their own vision of the good life, to the extent that it doesn't infringe on others' equal freedom to do the same.

The provision of basic goods like education, healthcare, and protection of free speech and free press is something I think we agree about. But beyond this, it becomes a tricky balancing act, since some visions of happiness are inherently exclusive of others. I can't hike through a beautiful forest if someone else would rather cut down the trees to sell for timber; I can't enjoy a skyline view if you decide to build a house right in front of my front window; I can't do what I choose with my own body if I have a uterus and the well-being of an embryo within it takes precedence over my desires.

The only workable way to resolve these conflicts is through the messy bargaining process of democracy. This bargaining can involve negotiating restrictions on our collective freedom to act, out of the recognition that it's good for everyone when there are some rights that we agree not to violate even by majority vote.

It's fallible, because we are fallible. It makes mistakes, because we make mistakes. But it's also self-correcting, because with time and hard-won experience, we learn what makes life better for everyone. And the great virtue of this is that it makes it possible for two people like you and me to live together in the same society, to work side-by-side, and to fight injustice wherever we see it—even if we disagree on comparatively minor details like whether there's a heaven or hell, a life after death, or a god who answers prayers. Until that next cup of coffee, I remain your correspondent and friend,

Adam

Bibliography

Abigail, James. "Pope Francis Wants to Change Two Major Catholic Laws He Sees as 'Archaic.'" Catholic.org. http://www.catholic.org/news/hf/faith/story.php?id=59123 (accessed July 31, 2016).

Albert, David. "On the Origin of Everything." NYTimes.com. http://www.nytimes.com/2012/03/25/books/review/a-universe-from-nothing-by-lawrence-m-krauss.html?_r=0 (accessed July 12, 2016).

Ammons, A. R. "Gravelly Run." In *The Selected Poems*, 11. New York: W. W. Norton, 1977.

Amsterdam, B. "Mirror Self-Image Reactions Before Age Two." *Developmental Psychobiology* 5.4 (1972) 297–305.

Aquinas, Thomas. *Summa Contra Gentiles*. http://dhspriory.org/thomas/ContraGentiles1.htm#7.

———. *Summa Theologica*. https://archive.org/stream/summatheologica0011thom/summatheologica0011thom_djvu.txt.

Aristotle. *Metaphysics*, Book I. http://classics.mit.edu/Aristotle/metaphysics.1.i.html.

———. *Politics*. http://classics.mit.edu/Aristotle/politics.7.seven.html.

Baggini, Julian, and Lawrence Krauss. "Philosophy v Science: Which Can Answer the Big Questions of Life?" Gaurdian.com. https://www.theguardian.com/science/2012/sep/09/science-philosophy-debate-julian-baggini-lawrence-krauss.

Baras, Zvi. "The Testimonium Flavianum and the Martyrdom of James." In *Josephus, Judaism and Christianity*, edited by Louis H. Feldman and Gōhei Hata, 338–48. Leiden: Brill, 1987.

Basebang, Jude Thaddeus Langeh. "Gandhi's Message to Christians". MKGhandi.org. http://www.mkgandhi.org/africaneedsgandhi/gandhi's_message_to_christians.htm (accessed January 19, 2016).

Brentano, Franz, and Tim Crane. *Psychology from an Empirical Standpoint*. London: Routledge, 2014.

Campbell, Richmond. "Moral Epistemology." *The Stanford Encyclopedia of Philosophy*. http://plato.stanford.edu/archives/spr2014/entries/moral-epistemology/ (accessed September 11, 2016).

Carroll, Sean. "Big Picture Part Six: Caring." PreposterousUniverse.com. http://www.preposterousuniverse.com/blog/2016/05/13/big-picture-part-six-caring/ (accessed July 27, 2016).

———. "On Determinism." PreposterousUniverse.com. http://www.preposterousuniverse.com/blog/2011/12/05/on-determinism/ (accessed September 11, 2016).

Bibliography

Centers for Disease Control and Prevention. "Chronic Disease Prevention and Health Promotion". CDC.gov. http://www.cdc.gov/chronicdisease/ (accessed January 19, 2016).

Chalmers, David. "Facing Up to the Problem of Consciousness." *Journal of Consciousness Studies* 2.3 (1995) 200–19.

Coyne, Jerry. "Sean Carroll on Free Will". WhyEvolutionisTrue.WordPress.com. https://whyevolutionistrue.wordpress.com/2011/12/06/sean-carroll-on-free-will-2/ (accessed January 21, 2016).

———. "Why You Don't Really Have Free Will". USAToday.com. http://usatoday30.usatoday.com/news/opinion/forum/story/2012-01-01/free-will-science-religion/52317624/1 (accessed January 21, 2016).

Craig, William. "The Problem of Evil." ReasonableFaith.org. http://www.reasonablefaith.org/the-problem-of-evil (Accessed April 16, 2016).

Crossan, John Dominic. *Jesus: A Revolutionary Biography*. San Francisco: Harper, 1994.

Davies, P. C. W. *The Mind of God: The Scientific Basis for a Rational World*. New York: Simon & Schuster, 1992.

Dawkins, Richard. *A Devil's Chaplain: Reflections on Hope, Lies, Science, and Love*. Boston: Houghton Mifflin Co., 2003.

———. Interview with Justin Brierley. *Unbelievable?* Premier Christian Radio, November 8, 2008. http://www.premierchristianradio.com/Shows/Saturday/Unbelievable/Episodes/Unbelievable-8-Nov-2008-Richard-Dawkins-John-Lennox-debate (accessed January 21, 2016).

———. *River Out of Eden: A Darwinian View of Life*. New York: Basic, 1995.

Dennett, Daniel. *Elbow Room: The Varieties of Free Will Worth Wanting*. Cambridge, MA: The MIT Press, 1984.

———. *Intuition Pumps and Other Tools for Thinking*. New York: W. W. Norton, 2013.

Descartes, Rene. *The Meditations and Selections from The Principles of Rene Descartes*. Translated by John Veitch. Chicago: Open Court, 1913.

Doherty, Earl. *The Jesus Puzzle: Did Christianity Begin With a Mythical Christ?* Ottawa: Canadian Humanist, 1999.

Draper, Paul. "The Problem of Evil." In *The Oxford Handbook of Philosophical Theology*, edited by Thomas Flint and Michael Rea, 332–51. Oxford: Oxford University Press, 2008.

Du Bois, William Edward Burghardt. *The Suppression of the African Slave-Trade to the United States of America 1638–1870*. New York: Longmans, Green, 1904.

Dunn, James D. G. *Jesus Remembered*. Grand Rapids: Eerdmans, 2003.

Eddy, Paul Rhodes, and Gregory Boyd. *The Jesus Legend: A Case for the Historical Reliability of the Synoptic Jesus Tradition*. Grand Rapids: Baker, 2007.

Ehrman, Bart. "Did Jesus Exist?" HuffingtonPost.com. http://www.huffingtonpost.com/bart-d-ehrman/did-jesus-exist_b_1349544.html (accessed October 10, 2015).

———. Interview with Reginald V. Finley Sr. "Who Changed the New Testament and Why," The Infidel Guy Show, 2008.

Espinoza, J., and A. F. Espinoza. "Pre-Eclampsia: A Maternal Manifestation of a Fetal Adaptive Response?" *Ultrasound in Obstetrics & Gynecology: The Official Journal of the International Society of Ultrasound in Obstetrics and Gynecology* 38.4 (2011) 367–70.

Evans, Craig A. *Jesus and His Contemporaries: Comparative Studies*. Boston: Brill, 2001.

Feinberg, Joel. *The Problem of Abortion*. California: Wadsworth, 1984.

Bibliography

Feldman, Louis H. "Flavius Josephus Revisited: The Man, His Writings, and His Significance." In *Aufstieg und Niedergang der römischen Welt: Geschichte und Kultur Roms im Spiegel der neueren Forschung*. Teil 2, Principat, Band 21, Halbband 2, Religion, edited by Hildegard Temporini and Wolfgang Haase, 763–862. Berlin: De Gruyter, 1984.

Feser, Edward. *The Last Superstition: A Refutation of the New Atheism*, 2008.

———. *Philosophy of Mind: A Beginner's Guide*. Oxford: Oneworld, 2006.

Flew, Anthony, and Roy Abraham Varghese. *There is a God: How the World's Most Notorious Atheist Changed His Mind*. New York: HarperOne, 2007.

Funk, Robert W. *The Gospel of Jesus: According to the Jesus Seminar*. Santa Rosa, CA: Polebridge, 1999.

Gabrielsen, Paul. "When Does Your Baby Become Conscious?" ScienceMag.org. http://www.sciencemag.org/news/2013/04/when-does-your-baby-become-conscious (Accessed January 23, 2016).

Garner, Richard. "Morality." *Philosophy Now* 82 (2011) 18–20. https://philosophynow.org/issues/82/Morality_The_Final_Delusion.

Gilson, Etienne. *God and Philosophy*. New Haven, CT: Yale University Press, 1941.

Giussani, Luigi, and John Zucchi. *The Religious Sense*. Montreal: McGill-Queen's University Press, 1997.

Gladwell, Malcolm. *The Tipping Point: How Little Things Can Make a Big Difference*. Boston: Little, Brown, 2000.

Goodenough, Ursula. *The Sacred Depths of Nature*. New York: Oxford University Press, 1998.

Gordon, John-Stewart. "Abortion." In *Internet Encyclopedia of Philosophy*. http://www.iep.utm.edu/abortion/ (accessed January 23, 2016).

Grabbe, Lester. "Jesus Who is Called the Christ: References to Jesus Outside Christian Sources." In *Is this Not the Carpenter?: The Question of the Historicity of the Figure of Jesus*, edited by Thomas Thompson and Thomas Verenna, 61–67. Durham, England: Acumen, 2013.

Grant, Michael. *Jesus*. London: Orion, 2004.

Greene, Joshua. *Moral Tribes: Emotion, Reason, and the Gap Between Us and Them*. New York: Penguin, 2013.

Güzeldere, Güven. "The Many Faces of Consciousness: A Field Guide." In *The Nature of Consciousness: Philosophical Debates*, edited by Ned Block, et al., 1–67. Cambridge, MA: MIT Press, 1997.

Habermas, Gary. "The Case for Christ's Resurrection." In *To Everyone an Answer: A Case for the Christian World View*, edited by Francis J. Beckwith, William Lane Craig, and J. P. Moreland, 180–98. Downers Grove, IL: InterVarsity, 2004.

———. "The Minimal Facts Approach to the Resurrection of Jesus: The Role of Methodology as a Crucial Component in Establishing History". GaryHabermas.com. http://www.garyhabermas.com/articles/southeastern_theological_review/minimal-facts-methodology_08-02-2012.htm (accessed October 11, 2015).

———. "A Short Life of Gary R. Habermas." GaryHabermas.com. http://www.garyhabermas.com/vitainnuce.htm (accessed October 11, 2015).

Haidt, Jonathan. "Moral Psychology and the Misunderstanding of Religion". Edge.org. http://edge.org/conversation/moral-psychology-and-the-misunderstanding-of-religion (accessed January 19, 2016).

Harris, Sam. *Free Will*. New York: Free Press, 2012.

Bibliography

———. *The Moral Landscape: How Science Can Determine Human Values*. New York: Free Press, 2010.

Hart, David Bentley. *The Experience of God: Being, Consciousness, Bliss*. New Haven, CT: Yale University Press, 2013.

Hawking, Stephen. *A Brief History of Time*. New York: Bantam, 1998.

Hawking, Stephen, and Leonard Mlodinow. *The Grand Design*. New York: Bantam, 2010.

Hitchens, Christopher, and Frank Turek. "Does God Exist?" Debate at Virginia Commonwealth University, September 8, 2008. http://hitchensdebates.blogspot.com/2010/11/hitchens-vs-turek-vcu.html (accessed November 16, 2016).

Howard, Robert. "Queen of the Black Coast." *Weird Tales* 23.5 (1934). http://gutenberg.net.au/ebooks06/0600961h.html.

Hume, David. *An Enquiry Concerning Human Understanding*. https://www.gutenberg.org/files/9662/9662-h/9662-h.htm.

Hurston, Zora Neale. *Dust Tracks on a Road*. New York: J. P. Lippincott, 1942.

Ingersoll, Robert. *The Works of Robert G. Ingersoll*, vol. 3. New York: Dresden, 1912.

Isaacson, Walter. *Einstein: His Life and Universe*. New York: Simon and Schuster, 2008.

Jacoby, Susan. *Freethinkers: A History of American Secularism*. New York: Owl, Henry Holt and Co, 2005.

Jaworski, William. *Philosophy of Mind: A Comprehensive Introduction*. Chichester, West Sussex: Wiley-Blackwell, 2011.

Jenkins, Jack. "Is Pope Francis Going to Let Priests Get Married?" ThinkProgress.org. www.thinkprogress.org/health/2014/07/14/3459644/pope-franics-priestly-celibacy/ (accessed July 31, 2016).

Johnson, Mary. *An Unquenchable Thirst: One Woman's Extraordinary Journey of Faith, Hope, and Clarity*. New York: Spiegel & Grau, 2011.

Josephus. *Antiquities of the Jews*, books 18–20. http://www.sacred-texts.com/jud/josephus/index.htm#aoj.

Joyce, Richard. "Moral Fictionalism." *Philosophy Now* 82 (2011) 14–17. https://philosophynow.org/issues/82/Moral_Fictionalism.

Keller, Timothy J. *The Reason for God: Belief in An Age of Skepticism*. New York: Dutton, 2008.

Kierkegaard, Soren. "On the Dedication to 'That Single Individual.'" http://www.ccel.org/k/kierkegaard/untruth/untruth.htm.

———. *Papers and Journals: A Selection*. Translated by Alastair Hannay. New York: Penguin, 1996.

King, Martin Luther, Jr. *Strength to Love*. Minneapolis: Fortress, 1977.

Köstenberger, Andreas J., L. Scott Kellum, and Charles L. Quarles. *The Cradle, the Cross, and the Crown: An Introduction to the New Testament*. Nashville, TN: B & H Academic, 2009.

Larmer, Robert. "Abortion, Personhood and the Potential for Consciousness." *Journal of Applied Philosophy* 12.3 (1995) 241–51.

Lee, Adam. "The Ineffable Carrot and the Infinite Stick." Patheos.com. http://www.patheos.com/blogs/daylightatheism/essays/the-ineffable-carrot-and-the-infinite-stick/ (accessed August 22, 2017).

———. "Statement of Principles." Patheos.com. http://www.patheos.com/blogs/daylightatheism/statement-of-principles/ (accessed July 8, 2016).

Bibliography

———. "Why Atheism is a Force for Good." Patheos.com. http://www.patheos.com/blogs/daylightatheism/2015/03/why-atheism-is-a-force-for-good/ (accessed July 8, 2016).

Lewis, C. S. *Mere Christianity: A Revised and Amplified Edition, with a New Introduction, of the Three Books, Broadcast Talks, Christian Behaviour, and Beyond Personality.* San Francisco: HarperSanFrancisco, 2001.

Livio, Mario. *Is God a Mathematician?* New York: Simon & Schuster, 2009.

Mackie, J. L. *The Miracle of Theism: Arguments For and Against the Existence of God.* Oxford: Clarendon, 1982.

Magee, Bryan. *Confessions of a Philosopher: A Personal Journey through Western Philosophy from Plato to Popper.* New York: Modern Library, 1999.

Marquis, Don. 1989. "Why Abortion is Immoral." *Journal of Philosophy* 86.4 (1989) 183–202.

Miller, B. L., et al. "Neuroanatomy of the Self: Evidence from Patients with Frontotemporal Dementia." *Neurology* 57.5 (2001) 817–21.

Felix, Minucius. *Octavius.* http://www.earlychristianwritings.com/octavius.html.

Nagel, Thomas. *Mind and Cosmos: Why the Materialist Neo-Darwinian Conception of Nature is Almost Certainly False.* New York: Oxford University Press, 2012.

———. "What Is It Like to Be a Bat?", *Philosophical Review* 83 (1974) 435–50.

Newberg, Andrew B. *The Metaphysical Mind: Probing the Biology of Philosophical Thought.* San Bernardino, CA: CreateSpace, 2014.

———. *Principles of Neurotheology.* Farnham, Surrey, England: Ashgate, 2010.

Newberg, Andrew B., Eugene G. D'Aquili, and Vince Rause. *Why God Won't Go Away: Brain Science and the Biology of Belief.* New York: Ballantine, 2001.

Kristof, Nicholas. "Wretched of the Earth." *The New York Review of Books.* http://www.nybooks.com/articles/2007/05/31/wretched-of-the-earth/ (accessed August 2, 2016).

Obama, Barack. "Call to Renewal, Keynote Address." *Sojourners*/Call to Renewal "Building a Covenant for a New America" Conference in Washington, DC, June 26, 2006. https://sojo.net/articles/transcript-obamas-2006-sojournerscall-renewal-address-faith-and-politics (accessed November 16, 2016).

Penrose, Roger. *The Emperor's New Mind: Concerning Computers, Minds and the Laws of Physics.* Oxford: Oxford University Press, 1999.

Pigliucci, Massimo. "Science and Fundamentalism." *EMBO Reports* 6.12 (2005) 1106–9.

Pinker, Steven. *The Better Angels of Our Nature: Why Violence Has Declined.* New York: Viking, 2011.

Plato. *The Republic,* Book VII. Translated by G. M. A. Grube. Revised by C. D. C. Reeve. Indianapolis: Hackett, 1992.

Popper, Karl. "Karl Popper on God: Interview with Edward Zerin." In *After the Open Society: Selected Social and Political Writings,* edited by Jeremy Shearmur and Piers Norris Turner, 48–52. London: Routledge, 2008.

Powell, Mark Allan. *Jesus as a Figure in History: How Modern Historians View the Man from Galilee.* Louisville: Westminster John Knox, 1998.

Pratchett, Terry. *Hogfather.* New York: HarperPrism, 1996.

———. *Night Watch.* New York: HarperCollins, 2002.

Prinz, Jesse. "Morality is a Culturally Conditioned Response." *Philosophy Now* 82 (2011) 6–9. https://philosophynow.org/issues/82/Morality_is_a_Culturally_Conditioned_Response.

Bibliography

Quinones, Sam. "Jesus Malverde." *PBS Frontline.* http://www.pbs.org/wgbh/pages/frontline/shows/drugs/business/malverde.html (accessed August 2, 2016).

Raffaele, Paul. "In John They Trust." *Smithsonian.* http://www.smithsonianmag.com/history/in-john-they-trust-109294882/ (accessed August 2, 2016).

Rose, Ernestine L. "A Defense of Atheism." In *Women Without Superstition: "No Gods—No Masters": The Collected Writings of Women Freethinkers of the Nineteenth and Twentieth Centuries*, edited by Annie Laurie Gaylor, 73–85. Madison: Freedom From Religion Foundation, 2012.

Rosenberg, Alexander. *The Atheist's Guide to Reality: Enjoying Life Without Illusions.* New York: W. W. Norton, 2011.

———. *Philosophy of Science: A Contemporary Introduction.* New York: Routledge, 2005.

———. "Why I am a Naturalist." NYTimes.com. http://opinionator.blogs.nytimes.com/2011/09/17/why-i-am-a-naturalist/?_r=0 (accessed October 16, 2015).

Ryle, Gilbert. *The Concept of Mind.* Chicago: University of Chicago Press, 1949.

Sacks, Oliver. "The Abyss." NewYorker.com http://www.newyorker.com/magazine/2007/09/24/the-abyss (accessed August 2, 2016).

Sagan, Carl. *Pale Blue Dot: A Vision of the Human Future in Space.* New York: Random House, 1994.

Sagan, Carl and Ann Druyan. "Is It Possible to be Pro-Life and Pro-Choice?" In *Billions & Billions: Thoughts on Life and Death at the Brink of the Millennium*, by Carl Sagan, 212–14. New York: Ballantine, 1997.

———. *Shadows of Forgotten Ancestors: A Search for Who We Are.* New York: Ballantine, 2001.

Schmelzer, Dave. *Not the Religious Type: Confessions of a Turncoat Atheist.* Carol Stream, IL: Tyndale, 2008.

Schrödinger, Erwin, *What is Life?* Cambridge: Cambridge University Press, 1992.

Searle, John R. *Mind, Language, and Society: Philosophy in the Real World.* New York: Basic, 2008.

Matulis, Sherry. "How I Earned My Feminist Credentials." In *Women Without Superstition: The Collected Writings of Women Freethinkers of the Nineteenth and Twentieth Centuries*, edited by Annie Laurie Gaylor, 543–550. Madison: Freedom from Religion Foundation, 2012.

Singer, Peter. "Ethics and Intuitions." *The Journal of Ethics* 9 (2005) 331–52.

———. *How Are We to Live?: Ethics in an Age of Self-Interest.* Amherst, NY: Prometheus, 2007.

———. *Practical Ethics.* Cambridge: Cambridge University Press, 2011.

Singer, Peter, et al. "Peter Singer: You Ask the Questions". Independent.co.uk. http://www.independent.co.uk/news/people/profiles/peter-singer-you-ask-the-questions-415524.html (accessed January 21, 2016).

Smith, Michael. "Realism." In *A Companion to Ethics*, edited by Peter Singer, 399–410. Oxford, UK: Blackwell Reference, 1991.

Street, Sharon. "Constructivism about Reasons." In *Oxford Studies in Metaethics, Volume 4*, edited by Russ Shafer-Landau, 207–45. Oxford: Clarendon, 2008.

Somashekhar, Sandhya, and Danielle Paquette. WashingtonPost.com. "Undercover Video Shows Planned Parenthood Official Discussing Fetal Organs Used for Research". https://www.washingtonpost.com/politics/undercover-video-shows-planned-parenthood-exec-discussing-organ-harvesting/2015/07/14/ae330e34-2a4d-11e5-bd33-395c05608059_story.html (accessed January 19, 2016).

Bibliography

Sullivan, Andrew. "Is Religion Built Upon Lies? Sam Harris vs. Andrew Sullivan." SamHarris.org. https://www.samharris.org/blog/item/sam-harris-vs.-andrew-sullivan (accessed August 2, 2016).

Tacitus. "Annals." http://classics.mit.edu/Tacitus/annals.html.

Tegmark, Max. *Our Mathematical Universe: My Quest for the Ultimate Nature of Reality.* New York: Vintage, 2014.

Van Voorst, Robert E. *Jesus Outside the New Testament: An Introduction to the Ancient Evidence.* Grand Rapids: Eerdmans, 2000.

———. "Jesus Tradition in Classic and Jewish Writings". In *Handbook for the Study of the Historical Jesus,* edited by Tom Holmén and Stanley E. Porter, 2149–82. Leiden: Brill, 2011.

Vermes, Geza. *Jesus in the Jewish World.* London: SCM, 2010.

Voltaire. *Philosophical Dictionary.* https://ebooks.adelaide.edu.au/v/voltaire/dictionary/chapter196.html.

Wansbrough, Henry. *Jesus and the Oral Gospel Tradition.* London: T & T Clark, 2004.

Warren, Mary Anne. "On the Moral and Legal Status of Abortion." In *The Problem of Abortion,* 2nd ed., edited by Joel Feinberg, 102–19. Belmont, CA: Wadsworth, 1984. Accessed online at https://pdfs.semanticscholar.org/579f/3c73009a691c72b4441831882c63dea931b2.pdf.

Wielenberg, Erik J. "In Defense of Non-Natural, Non-Theistic Moral Realism." *Faith and Philosophy* 26 (2009) 23–41.

Wigner, Eugene P. "The Unreasonable Effectiveness of Mathematics in the Natural Sciences. Richard Courant Lecture in Mathematical Sciences delivered at New York University, May 11, 1959." *Communications on Pure and Applied Mathematics* 13 (1960) 1–14.

Williamson, Timothy. "Naturalism and Its Limits." NYTimes.com. http://opinionator.blogs.nytimes.com/2011/09/04/what-is-naturalism/ (accessed October 16, 2015).

Wright, Frances. *Course of Popular Lectures as Delivered by Frances Wright in New York, Philadelphia and other Cities of the United States. With three addresses on Public Occasions, and a Reply to the Charges Against the French Reformers of 1789.* New York: G. W. & A. J. Matsell, 1829.